UNDERSTANDING
SUSAN SONTAG

D1596432

UNDERSTANDING

SUSAN SONTAG

Carl Rollyson

THE UNIVERSITY OF
SOUTH CAROLINA PRESS

© 2016 University of South Carolina

Hardback and ebook editions published by the University of South Carolina Press, 2016
Paperback edition published in Columbia, South Carolina,
by the University of South Carolina Press, 2020

www.uscpress.com

Manufactured in the United States of America

29 28 27 26 25 24 23 22 21 20
10 9 8 7 6 5 4 3 2 1

Library of Congress Cataloging-in-Publication Data for the
hardback and ebook editions can be found at http://catalog.loc.gov/.

ISBN 978-1-61117-680-3 (hardback)
ISBN 978-1-61117-681-0 (ebook)
ISBN 978-1-64336-091-1 (paperback)

CONTENTS

SERIES EDITOR'S PREFACE

The Understanding Contemporary American Literature series was founded by the estimable Matthew J. Bruccoli (1931–2008), who envisioned these volumes as guides or companions for students as well as good nonacademic readers, a legacy that will continue as new volumes are developed to fill in gaps among the nearly one hundred series volumes published to date and to embrace a host of new writers only now making their marks on our literature.

As Professor Bruccoli explained in his preface to the volumes he edited, because much influential contemporary literature makes special demands, "the word understanding in the titles was chosen deliberately. Many willing readers lack an adequate understanding of how contemporary literature works; that is, of what the author is attempting to express and the means by which it is conveyed." Aimed at fostering this understanding of good literature and good writers, the criticism and analysis in the series provide instruction in how to read certain contemporary writers—explicating their material, language, structures, themes, and perspectives—and facilitate a more profitable experience of the works under discussion.

In the twenty-first century Professor Bruccoli's prescience gives us an avenue to publish expert critiques of significant contemporary American writing. The series continues to map the literary landscape and to provide both instruction and enjoyment. Future volumes will seek to introduce new voices alongside canonized favorites, to chronicle the changing literature of our times, and to remain, as Professor Bruccoli conceived, contemporary in the best sense of the word.

Linda Wagner-Martin, Series Editor

CHAPTER 1

Understanding Susan Sontag

Susan Sontag (1933–2004) was born in New York City and grew up in Tucson and Los Angeles, the daughter of Jack Rosenblatt, who owned a trading company in China. She thought of him as a departed merchant prince who died in China when she was only five years old. Mildred Jacobson Rosenblatt, Sontag's mother, then married a highly decorated Air Force officer, Nathan Sontag. Susan took her stepfather's name, as did her younger sister, Judith. With family connections to both Asia and Europe, even as she acclimated to the wide-open spaces of the West, Sontag, a precocious child, spent time in her Tucson back-yard digging a hole to China.[1] While her father was still alive, the family based itself in a New York hotel—just one of many temporary abodes that seemed to forecast the fate of a peripatetic writer who saw herself as belonging less to any country than to the world itself, where she would go questing just like Richard Halliburton, her favorite author-adventurer.[2] That such a life and career would bring much unhappiness as well as fulfillment occurred to Sontag while she was quite young and already noting her joys and disaffections in her diaries.

Sontag grew up reading the biography of Marie Curie, a Pole who sought her life's work and acquired fame in France—exactly where Sontag arrived in her formative years as a writer after earning an undergraduate degree at the University of Chicago and a master's degree at Harvard University. Like Curie, who bound herself to a mate, her fellow scientist Pierre Curie, Sontag at the age of seventeen married the sociologist Philip Rieff, with whom she collaborated on a book about Freud's contribution to western civilization. But both the traditional boundaries of academic life, and the conventional obligations of marriage, chafed an ambitious woman who was also aware, at quite a young age, that a so-called normal, heterosexual, and university-driven existence was not for her—even though into her thirties she still contemplated completing her Ph.D.

At nineteen, Sontag gave birth to a son, David Rieff, over whom she would lavish not a maternal care so much as the attachment of a sibling, like that of a sister for her younger brother. This unorthodox parenting was of a piece with her ambition to create a body of work that would challenge the pieties of American culture, the canons of literary study, and the traditional role of the public intellectual. Although she immersed herself in the bohemianism of Greenwich Village, she very quickly sought public platforms that overturned the alienated artist's scorn for mainstream fame. Even as Sontag professed to abjure the very notion of careerism and popularity, she cultivated an appearance and personal style accentuated in photographs with a dramatic Hollywood gloss calculated to invite mass media attention, which began when *Time* magazine featured an account of her groundbreaking essay "Notes on 'Camp,'" published in the *Partisan Review* (whose circulation was no more than ten thousand). Her appeal to both the literary elite and to a much broader literate audience in the 1960s broke new ground in the way so-called high and low culture were beginning to converge.

Sontag embodied the contradictions of her time—at once a serious and sometimes abstruse thinker and yet a highly quotable writer whose words made good newspaper copy. She distilled her insights into epigrams and epithets that popular publications could build stories around. The titles of her first books, such as *Against Interpretation* and *Styles of Radical Will,* were provocative and prescriptive. What Sontag described in essays—such as the spontaneous events called "Happenings"—she also made into required reading for anyone wanting to keep abreast of what was current and urgent in American culture. At the same time, she evaded the label of critic and functioned as a kind of impresario of the avant-garde and a practitioner, producing two experimental novels, *The Benefactor* and *Death Kit,* which established her credentials as a modernist akin to the European authors such as Alain Robbe-Grillet and Nathalie Sarraute, whom she wrote about in essays that extolled their efforts to subvert traditional narratives and novelistic conventions. Her early films *Duet for Cannibals* and *Brother Carl,* which she wrote and directed in Sweden, were inspired by the work of Ingmar Bergman, especially *Persona,* the topic of one of Sontag's signature essays touting the superior European probing of modern identity. Her later play *Alice in Bed* completed her highly self-conscious effort to conflate feminism and modernism in scenes that explored the lives of Alice James and Emily Dickinson.

In the economy of publishing, Sontag was the total package—essayist, novelist, playwright and filmmaker—kept in print and aggressively marketed abroad by her publisher, Farrar, Straus and Giroux. She, in turn, amplified her authority by appearing on panel discussions, delivering public lectures, and joining protests against the Vietnam War and against social injustice. In this respect, she was like her European models, Jean-Paul Sartre, Simone de Beauvoir, and Albert Camus, who defined the public intellectual as one who stood apart from governmental authority, even though, like other writers of her generation, Sontag enjoyed her share of State Department junkets to Europe when she was not managing her own dissenter's trips to Hanoi and later to Sarajevo, where, in her view, the fate of Western Civilization was being worked out.

Sontag benefited as well from the women's movement of the 1970s, even though she declared her independence from movement politics in her attack on Leni Riefenstahl, who had become, in Sontag's view, a feminist icon notwithstanding her fascist aesthetics. Sontag also angered a generation of leftists in her controversial Town Hall speech in 1982 when she described Communism as "Fascism with a human face." In effect, she was repudiating many of her own political causes, including her championing of Communist Cuba and North Vietnam. She stood out from groups and organizations, and yet she also solidified her public persona in her role as president of the American PEN Center. Her assumption of such an office signaled the later phase of her career, in which she eschewed her earlier concerns with popular culture and accelerated her missionary fervor for guiding elite tastes in literature as featured by her publisher, Farrar, Straus and Giroux, highly regarded for its publication of European authors, many of them Nobel Prize winners.

Sontag's position as a kind of intellectual arbiter reached an apogee with the publication of *On Photography* (1977) and *Illness as Metaphor* (1978), the former poised exquisitely between the claims of photography as a craft or art, and the latter repudiating the mythology of disease as a manifestation of the human psyche, a mythology she replaced with a bracing reliance on the science of human biology and the rational explanation of disease as cells gone wrong. These two books increased her stature as a touchstone figure in discussions of medical ethics and aesthetic standards. Her work also made her a target for those with contrary views, who termed her arguments rebarbative because she refused to consider either the possible psychic roots of sickness or the psychology of the artist.

Under the Sign of Saturn signaled her narrowing focus on creative nonfiction writers like Walter Benjamin and Elias Canetti, whom she extolled in the old eighteenth/nineteenth-century man-of-letters mode. These essays produced a quasi-biographical/critical approach rendered in cerebral narratives that foreshadowed her discursive novel *The Volcano Lover,* an account of the famous Admiral Nelson–Sir William Hamilton–Emma Hamilton triangle.

History, never a very important category in Sontag's earlier taxonomic essays, became paramount as she began to rewrite her literary past, returning to the subject of photography in *Regarding the Pain of Others*, for example, but also subsuming her own autobiography in another novel, *In America*, the story of a nineteenth-century Polish actress and her encounter with a new land, especially the California of Sontag's youth.

Sontag spent her last years writing novels and attempting to avoid the kind of essay work that many critics still believe is her greatest achievement. But she nevertheless worked on a final book of nonfiction prose that would sum up and amplify her aesthetic, moral, and political positions. The books published about her after her death reckon with her as a public intellectual and as a powerful personality who made herself a cynosure of contemporary culture. Indeed, her most lasting achievement may well be this conception of her as a sensibility attuned to the widest possible vision of the modern writer, a vision she explored with singular tenacity and provocation, if not always with the kind of rigor expected of professional philosopher, critic, or aesthetician. Her aphoristic way of defining issues and bringing them to a point of acute consciousness seems, in the final analysis, her most impressive accomplishment.

CHAPTER 2

Writer

Early Novels and Essays

Although Susan Sontag was formally trained as a philosopher and literary critic, neither term ever suited her. She preferred the designation of writer—to her an honorific title that reflected her aspirations to create works of literature that included novels, stories, and plays. She ranked her essays as a lower category of composition, as a kind of public service but not as part of an enduring legacy that she hoped would distinguish her in the art of fiction. Most critics have nevertheless considered her essays to be her most significant contribution to the world of modern letters.

To understand Sontag's own sense of her literary mission, it is important to begin with her decision to publish her first book-length prose as a novel. For her, the decision to write fiction was a bold undertaking. Nothing in her previous education had prepared her to be a creative artist. At the University of Chicago, she had spent a semester critiquing Joseph Conrad's novel *Victory*, and at Harvard she had taken master's degree courses in literature, but this work prepared her to be a critic, an analyst, not a writer of narrative prose. Her graduate work at Oxford and then at the Sorbonne extended her understanding of philosophy. At Columbia University in the early 1960s, she taught philosophy and the history of religion.

What, then, prompted her to write fiction—other than her very early and precocious reading of authors such as Thomas Mann and Jack London? Mann had left Germany before World War II and had become an influential public voice in America and London, the author of *Martin Eden*, a novel about the heroism of the writing life, inspired her as yet inchoate dreams of becoming an author. Her sojourn in France in 1957–58 seems to have stimulated an overweening ambition to project her deep learning into novels that had little precedent in American literature but which she saw as a vital aspect of European fiction. Thomas Mann's *The Magic Mountain,* which combined the story of a young hero, Hans Castorp, with a profound probing of the nature of civilization itself, had powerfully affected the teenage Sontag. Reading Mann's novel took her out of what she considered her provincial upbringing in Arizona and California and put her in touch with the main currents of European culture. Similarly, the world-traveling Jack London, the very model of a writer who lived by his own wits, demonstrated how the individual could triumph over all kinds of unpromising circumstances—even though his eponymous hero ultimately commits suicide. Art was worth living and dying for, the young Sontag concluded. But with no mentor in college encouraging her to write fiction, she applied herself to an academic understanding of literature and philosophy. And as she later confessed, she was in a hurry to grow up, and that meant, to begin with, marrying and establishing her own family and household.

At Oxford, toward the end of 1957, Sontag began to realize that a conventional career in higher education would not fulfill her highest ambitions—that, in fact, saddling herself to employment in an academic institution might very well extinguish any talent she had as a creative artist. She would continue to teach courses in the early 1960s in order to earn a living, but her ultimate goal was to succeed as an independent public intellectual and, even more important, as a writer.

In Paris at the beginning of 1958, she began to meet and to observe a wide range of Europeans and Americans living as artists. She went to hear Simone de Beauvoir lecture. And Sontag began reading contemporary French novelists like Alain Robbe-Grillet and Natalie Saurrate, who challenged conventional narratives depending on character development, plot, and theme. The realistic novel, as then written in Europe and America, seemed moribund to them—and to Sontag, who believed that fiction should not mimic or simply represent reality but should, rather, create its own worlds and ideas. Indeed, reality as a concept seemed to her artificial, an agreed-upon convention that merely replicated the status quo. For Sontag, fiction had to be adventurous and innovative.

So Sontag began to imagine a novel with the working title "Dreams of Hippolyte," eventually published as *The Benefactor.* But instead of creating a young first-person narrator for readers to identify with—as so many authors of the bildungsroman do, she took on the voice of a sixty-one-year-old aesthete attempting to live in his dreams, or at least to construct a life that followed the logic of his dreams. The result is displacement. Although Paris seems to be the capital city he resides in, the city is never named—perhaps because what the novel rejects is a spurious specificity. What does it matter, in the end, where exactly Hippolyte lives, since he does not feel bound by place and time but only by his imagination? His quest to jettison everything that is jejune in favor of the originality of his own conceptions is apparently a thrilling possibility that Sontag expected would beguile her readers—as it did for some of her contemporaries. But it is virtually impossible to empathize with what Hippolyte actually does, when, for example, he sells his lover, Frau Anders, into slavery. Or is this just a dream too, since, as in a dream, she returns after she has been seemingly dispatched for good? Sontag told an interviewer that she purposely kept open many different interpretations of what is real in the novel—that is, of what actually happens and what Hippolyte dreams as happening. That it is impossible to draw a sharp distinction between dreams and reality is both what makes the novel tantalizing and frustrating.

By decoupling himself from conventional norms, Hippolyte does indeed become independent of society, but at tremendous cost to himself. Even as Sontag wanted to create antirealistic fiction, she seems to have understood that Hippolyte was the reductio ad absurdum of her own desire to repudiate traditional civilization along with the norms of story telling. In this respect, the novel seems to cancel itself out, so to speak, undermining the very quest that has motivated Hippolyte to tell his story. French critic Michel Mohrt characterized Sontag's narrator as suffering from a "sickness of self-love," writing a narrative akin to Borges's narratives of a fable-like purity.[1]

Although the influence of the French new novel has often been discussed in accounts of *The Benefactor*, Sontag pointed to the impact of *Epitaph of a Small Winner* by Portuguese novelist Machado de Assis on her choice of a male narrator's retrospective on his life as a dream, which, in her words, permitted a "display of mental agility and inventiveness which is designed to amuse the reader and which purportedly reflects the liveliness of that narrator's mind," but which "mostly measures how emotionally isolated and forlorn the narrator is." She also explained why a male narrator was necessary: "a woman with the same degree of mental acuity and emotional separateness would be regarded as simply a monster."[2] That observation is especially telling in the light of a remark from one of Sontag's lovers in the documentary *Regarding Susan Sontag* that Sontag lacked the ability to empathize with the feelings of others close to her. To select a female narrator, then, would jeopardize the novel's independence if readers associate the narrative voice directly with Sontag.

Reviews of Sontag's novel noted its anti-psychological bias—that, in Granville Hicks's words, "personality is mysterious."[3] Sontag's evocation of the self in a labyrinthine world called up comparisons to Kafka.[4] While few first responses to the novel seemed enthusiastic, Robert M. Adams in the *New York Review of Books* seemed quite taken with Sontag's portrayal of a "mind lost in its own intricate dialectic" and compared her work to *Candide,* although he concluded that Sontag lacked Voltaire's "sharp sword of comedy."[5]

Some critics viewed Hippolyte as a Poe-like narrator, mad all along, as Stephen Koch argued.[6] Alfred Kazin detected a tactic employed in women's fiction: an "inordinate defensiveness against a society conceived as the special enemy of the sensitive." Hippolyte's "detached consciousness" becomes his antidote to society's norms—but an antidote that becomes lethal since it led to self-destruction.[7] That insight seems, again, to refer back to Poe, whose narrators evince a sense of superiority even as the stories they tell result in their doom. Bruce Bassoff attributed this self-negation to a repudiation of the individual's role in history—an especially intriguing observation given Sontag's later turn toward the historical novel.[8] Barbara Ching and Jennifer A. Wagner-Lawlor call the novel a "dead end," a youthful disguise of what Sontag "finally allows to emerge from her thought and writing: faith in art, and a commitment to changing the world with art"[9]—a position that neither Sontag nor her narrator Hippolyte broach as even a possibility.

The more immediate impact of *The Benefactor* on Sontag herself seems to have been, as critic Bernard F. Rodgers Jr., notes, the confirmation of her belief that an "'unceasing self-consciousness' that Hippolyte embodies, the 'hypertrophy of intellect at the expense of energy and sensual capability' was the 'classical dilemma' of advanced bourgeois civilization." His verdict on this ambitious novel seems just. If it is too long, too "self-consciously literary," and "too repetitive," it is not, as Ted Solotaroff claimed, simply "all literature" and "lifeless." The novel's distinctive narrative voice remains intriguing and propels the reader, as it did Sontag herself, into producing some of her most memorable and perceptive essays.[10]

Against Interpretation, which appeared in early 1966, blasted Sontag out of *The Benefactor*'s solipsism and into a fully engaged and panoramic account of the current cultural scene. The book contains twenty-six essays, culled from the several dozen she published between 1961 and 1965. Section I presents her critical credo in "Against Interpretation" and "On Style"; section II concerns her studies of artists, critics, philosophers, and anthropologists; section III gives her take on modern drama; section IV offers her dissection of film (science fiction, the avant-garde, and the European New Wave); and section V presents her evocation of the new sensibility as exemplified in camp and Happenings. This astonishing array of subjects, presented with great authority and panache, constituted, in effect, a revamped *Partisan Review,* the influential journal Sontag had grown up admiring. Reading *Against Interpretation* was like enrolling in a curriculum that includes philosophy, aesthetics, literary and film criticism, biographical profiles, arts journalism, and science. It became possible, in other words, to major in Susan Sontag. All at once, she was, in herself, a school of liberal arts—even taking issue with C. P. Snow's famous argument that sciences and the arts had split off from one another. Not so, said Sontag, in exhilarating prose. On the contrary, the arts were as much the province of discovery as was science, and scientists and artists were making common cause in what she deemed the "new sensibility." She was learned, but she was also iconoclastic. She took a studied view of art, and yet there she was reporting on the latest trends. Putting these occasional pieces in a book also codified them, creating a kind of canon of the au courant.

In two widely quoted essays, "Against Interpretation" and "On Style," Sontag takes on the history of literary criticism, considering whether art is mimetic (imitative), with a content that reflects the world outside itself, or expressive—sufficient unto itself with a form that is the product of the artist's imagination. These distinctions she traces to Plato and Aristotle and to a tension always present between content and form, between thinking of art as making a statement about the world and art as its own experience, valued in and for itself. Sontag favors a criticism that appreciates the contours of the artwork rather than searches it for some exportable message relating to the world outside itself. And yet there are times, she concedes, when a concern with content, with what a work of art is saying, is crucial because art, left to its own devices, can become a species of the solipsistic and self-regarding that condemns characters in her fiction like Hippolyte to a life-denying isolation.

In "On Style," Sontag argues that "style and content are insoluble," even if, in practice, critics speak of certain styles such as Mannerism and Art Nouveau as if they are separable from the content they convey. In other words, the work of art is a form of knowledge, not a container of knowledge about something that is not itself. As a result, a work of art cannot be judged in terms of the morality of any particular culture or historical period. Art is self-justifying. It is not surprising, then, that in the next essay, "The Artist as Exemplary Sufferer," she praises Cesare Pavese's fiction and diaries for their "self-cancellation" so that his work becomes an exploration of subjects such as modern love and suicide in terms of the work of others and not simply a product of his own psychology. Similarly, Simone Weil is celebrated as the self-abnegating artist, full of "intellectual ardor," and committed to an investigation of truth above all so that she becomes a saint of the "aesthetic," because her person becomes less important than her work. Sontag's understanding of the aesthetic is clarified in her portrayal of Camus in his notebooks, which express a "moral beauty"—two words that encapsulate Sontag's notion of an art intact in itself, so exquisitely perfect that it is true in the sense of creating its own authority, its rightness. Sontag does speak of Camus the man, whom she seems to conflate with the artist because of his nobility, his acts (such as joining the French Resistance and denouncing the Communist Party) that are taken without consideration for his own wellbeing or safety. In effect, she suggests that Camus's life, like his work, is of a piece, a unity that is art.

Sontag selects writers like Michel Leiris for their refutation of the Romantic idea of the writer and of writing as a form of self-expression. Unlike Montaigne, Leiris's confessional writing undermines his own authority and questions whether the writer can understand himself. He is the opposite of a writer like Norman Mailer, whose manhood is bound to the idea of the heroic self. Leiris is the writer as antihero, "hermetic and opaque" and even bored with himself. Like her portrayal of Leiris, her depiction of anthropologist Claude Lévi-Straus emphasizes his resistance to empathy and the "psychological ordeal" he experiences in his study of other cultures. He resists the inclination to identify with the societies he studies, preferring to observe, in the manner of a Sontag-defined artist, the forms that certain societies take. He remains aloof, an outsider.

Lévi-Strauss is, in effect, the alienated artist celebrated in so many of Sontag's essays, which also include critics like Georg Lukács, although she deplores his moralizing, which tends to subvert the autonomy of art. A truer exile intent on expressing his art in the very face of a hostile society was Jean Genet, whom Sontag attempts to rescue from Sartre's biography because the philosopher tried to turn Genet into an exemplification of Sartre's own style of political engagement. Sontag's Genet is less assimilated, more of an outcast, an "other," than in Sartre's narrative.

In "Nathalie Sarraute and the Novel," Sontag sees another writer resistant to psychology, to the personalizing of literature, and to the contrived plots and characters of fiction, favoring—to use one of Sontag's favorite phrases— "sensory pleasures." In this view of art, the writer becomes, as in T. S. Eliot's "Tradition and the Individual Talent," a vessel that produces work that is more than and other than herself.

In a rare departure from Sontag's customary practice, she writes a negative review of Eugene Ionesco's writing about theater—perhaps because she finds his theories simplistic, contradictory, and all too characteristic of his superficial plays, which she deems anti-intellectual. Sontag abandoned reviewing plays early in her career because she felt uncomfortable rendering judgments required of reviewers. Although she had reservations about *The Deputy*, a play set in the Nazi era, she was attracted to its staging, which, on the one hand, seems to suggest that the personalities of those attracted to Nazism are not as important as the roles they function in and, on the other hand, presents two main characters whose opposition to Nazism demonstrates their uniqueness. In like fashion, in "The Death of Tragedy," she objects to critic Lionel Abel's term "metatheatre" to describe the self-conscious productions of playwrights since Shakespeare. To use one term like metatheatre to encompass Genet, Beckett, and Brecht is to distort the history of western drama, she concludes.

Not surprisingly, in "Going to the Theatre, Etc." Sontag deplores Arthur Miller's concern with the Holocaust and Communism in *After the Fall* because they are represented primarily as part of the "furniture of a mind" (141)—in this case of the play's narrator, Quentin, who treats all issues on the same level and thus makes them indistinguishable. In general, she excoriates contemporary drama for its political optimism and inability to deal with tragedy and to make of race issues melodramas about "virtue and vice" (150). In contrast to these formulaic productions, she touts Peter Brook's production of *Marat/ Sade,* a play of ideas with "intellectual debate" as the "material of the play . . . not its subject or its end" (165).

In "Spiritual Style in the Films of Robert Bresson," Sontag fairly revels in a filmmaker who refuses audiences the pleasure of identifying with his characters because, as is her predilection, she prefers art that does not cater to the audience's desire to convert what is seen on the screen into the psychology of human character, a psychology that seems to Sontag spurious because it is an "affront to the mystery that is human action and the human heart" (181). It is the movement, the physics, so to speak, of Bresson's films that fascinates her. It is not the drama but the composition of Bresson's works that impress. Jean-Luc Godard epitomizes this resistance to art as explanatory, to making coherent what is in fact fragmentary. She fastens on the word "disburdenment" to describe Godard's dissociation of word and image, making it impossible to construct a neat orchestration of images, sounds, and words. His films do not refer to any world outside of themselves and hence he is due the honor of being the "first director fully to grasp the fact that, in order to deal seriously with ideas, one must create a new film language" (207).

In "The Imagination of Disaster," one of Sontag's most influential essays, she discounts the value of the "science" to be found in science fiction films and likens them to horror movies, except that the former deal more lucidly with power, destruction, and violence. Such films can be moralistic (condemning the mad scientist), but they also reflect contemporary anxieties about the state of the world and the role of technology in dehumanizing society. To what extent such films serve a therapeutic function is disputable, in Sontag's reading, since too often the failings of the world are attributable to individuals and not to systematic problems. What comes through in this essay, however, is Sontag's enjoyment of these films and her delight in anatomizing their characteristics. The essay is one of her better excursions in sharing with her readers the pleasures of the art she extolls precisely for its pleasure-giving properties.

Similarly, Sontag is an unabashed admirer of films like *Flaming Creatures,* a work that some dismiss as pornography but which she praises for its enthusiasm and wit. It also has a child-like exuberance that she finds liberating because of an "extraordinary charge and beauty" (228) in its images. Sexuality of all kinds romps through this picture, creating what Sontag calls an "aesthetic space, the space of pleasure" (231). In sum, she finds the moral argument against pornography, if indeed the film is pornographic, irrelevant. The ostensible subject matter—transvestitism—is the occasion for the film's existence but should not be seen as its raison d'être.

Resnais's *Muriel* is harder to like, Sontag implies, because it is undramatic and with a story that decomposes. Rather than drawing the viewer into the film, the director seems to deliberately divert attention from the elaborate plot, suggesting that the true subject cannot be assimilated. But, as Sontag concedes, such a film is hard to endure because it refuses to come to a resolution or to pursue its ideas with vigor and tenacity. Other Resnais films, such as *Night and Fog,* are more successful since his oblique treatment of the subject matter (the liberation of the Nazi concentration camps) actually makes the film more powerful as there is no need to compel our feelings.

In discussing Resnais, Sontag invokes the French new novel and its subversion of conventional narrative, which she follows with "A Note on Novels and Films," showing how both forms of art have experimented with narration, with different kinds of films—literary and visual, psychological and anti-psychological, descriptive and expository. In effect, then, motion pictures are a way of reading the history of the novel and its acceptance and rejection of popular tastes and sentiments.

What makes *Against Interpretation* so impressive is Sontag's remarkable segues not only from one art to another but to philosophy and religion as well, examining in "Piety without Content" Walter Kaufmann's study of religion's decline—a subject in which Sontag, who studied the history of religion at Harvard and taught courses on at Columbia, was well versed. She disputes Kaufmann's argument that the feelings that religion evokes can survive without religion itself: "one cannot be religious in general any more than one can speak language in general" (252), Sontag counters. Religion is rooted in the world in very specific ways that do not make it portable or transferrable to a secular world, and intellectual confusion results when trying to import the values of religion into modern beliefs.

To follow a discussion of religion with a dissection of Freud and psycho-analysis brings Sontag back to contemporary America, "anxious, television-brainwashed" (259)—sweeping terms that overburden her historical and political analyses. She deplores the American tendency to emphasize those aspects of Freud that reinforce conformism to societal norms, and yet she finds a thinker like Herbert Marcuse, who tries to reconcile Marxism and Freudian-ism, closer to revolutionary thought. She is attracted to Norman O. Brown's *Life Against Death* because of its effort to liberate psychology from the Freud-ian obsession with repression. Indeed, the next essay, on "Happenings," with its interest in the unpredictable and focus on the present, seems an antidote to Freud's concern with the past that shapes the psyche. The undermining of con-ventional certitudes suggests a subversive intent that Sontag seems to welcome but also distances herself from when she notes the demonic nature of some Happenings that turn upon and even attack the audience.

"Notes on 'Camp,'" Sontag's most famous essay in *Against Interpretation,* is a miniature of the book's tendency to take a taxonomic view of art—in this case by creating fifty-eight numbered points. The first two become the basis for an impressive array of examples that shore up her observations:

> To start very generally: Camp is a certain mode of aestheticism. It is one way of seeing the world as an aesthetic phenomenon. That way, the way of Camp, is not in terms of beauty, but in terms of the degree of artifice, of stylization. To emphasize style is to slight content, or to introduce an at-titude which is neutral with respect to content. It goes without saying that the Camp sensibility is disengaged, depoliticized—or at least apolitical.

There follows lists of films, novels, plays, objects, and so on that are camp items—that is, they are valued for their style, shape, manner of presentation. Thus, Tiffany lamps, *Swan Lake,* and *King Kong* are all included in the camp camp, so to speak. For this way of regarding the world focuses on how that world makes itself up, not on what the world amounts to. Perhaps this distrust of finding a message, of reducing art to a conclusion, is best summed up in Sontag's quotation from a character in *The Nihilists:* "Life is too important a thing ever to talk seriously about it" (286). The great value of camp, in Sontag's view, is that it liberates art from the dictates of social and political thought; the liability of camp, as she also understands quite well, is that it cannot engage with social and political thought and cannot, as a result, make art count for anything outside itself.

No matter what position a reviewer might take toward her work, Son-tag cannot be dismissed. She writes in such a way that commentators are compelled to argue for or against her. In this respect, it hardly matters whether she is deemed right or wrong. Arguments often begin by quoting her out of a need to either borrow her authority or challenge it. A reader could come away from *The Benefactor* never wanting to read it again, but the words of *Against Interpretation* continue to reverberate precisely because, unlike Hippolyte, Sontag's words touch on so many cultural indicators. An astute connoisseur, Sontag rarely engages in the critic's desire to hand out grades, specifying the degree to which a work of art succeeds or fails; instead, her judgments are implicit in the very intensity of her interest in a writer, a work, or a cultural event. She opens the way for appreciation; she rarely closes down thinking about a subject. She pays attention and, in the act of observing, expresses her avidity for art; and avidity, her son and editor suggests, is the word that best sums up his mother.[11]

Sontag's main points—that the intellect had come to dominate discussions of art and had therefore diminished the enjoyment of art as a sensual experience, and that seeking out the content (message) of art had obscured the pleasure of appreciating the artist's creation of form—received mixed reviews. Critics praised her fresh, vigorous prose while suggesting, with some irony, that Sontag, too, was presenting an argument or interpretation of art, even if she refused to critique individual works. Some reviewers, like Burton Feldman in the *Denver Quarterly,* thought her distinctions were overwrought. Many critics welcomed her quest to expunge moralizing from literary and art criticism. From the vantage point of 1996, Sontag herself seemed less concerned with the extent to which her arguments held up than to note that her book was an attack on the philistines—those who would use art for their own purposes rather than valuing it for its own sake. She wanted, as always, art to be untamed and not subordinate to criteria outside itself.

Sontag's favorite ploy in *Against Interpretation* is to discuss one work of art in terms of another, or many others. The range of her cultural references is bewildering to all but the most highly educated readers, and though the effect of allusions to so many other writers and works is, in Bernard Rodgers's words, "staggering," he is right to say that she is doing much more than "namedropping. . . . Susan Sontag is not simply familiar with the work of all these figures, but knows them thoroughly enough to select exactly the right work from the *oeuvre* of any one of them to make her point." Coupled with this encyclopedic knowledge is, as Rodgers also notes, her aphoristic style, which allows her to sum up her ideas in pithy phrases: "Interpretation is the revenge of intellect upon art" (7); "Style is the principle of decision in a work of art, the signature of the artist's will" (32). If the reader is not familiar with all of her allusions to artists, writers, and works of art and philosophy, the nub of her argument is nevertheless close to hand in her epigrams.

The tension in Sontag's own thinking about art is encapsulated in a later essay, "Fascinating Fascism," in which she takes issue with her own contention that Leni Riefenstahl's *Triumph of the Will* could be appreciated aside from its fascist politics. In Sontag's own course correction, she came to believe that a work of art's form could not so easily be disengaged from its content. Or, to put it another way, she could not simply divide into two separate categories fascism and aesthetics but rather felt compelled to insist on such a thing as fascist aesthetics, a term that fuses content and form in ways she resisted in *Against Interpretation.*

But in the late 1960s Sontag remained committed to creating an art not bound by the categories of history or morality. In *Against Interpretation,* she defends Norman Mailer's *An American Dream,* even though reviewers had complained about his protagonist, Stephen Rojack, who gets away with murdering his wife. It is a novel that does not purport to promulgate or repudiate a standard of morality, she insists. Sontag herself wants to go even further than Mailer in detaching the novel not only from morality but also from the conventions of realism. Although Diddy, her main character in *Death Kit,* is a businessman traveling by train from Manhattan to Albany, much of what the narrative presents seems like a dream, a patently Freudian one at that, since his journey is halted in a tunnel, literally blocking him from the light of day. His altercation with a workman on the railroad tracks ends with Diddy murdering him with a crowbar. When he returns to the train, he has sex with a blind woman, Hester, who insists that Diddy has never left the train compartment. Diddy accompanies Hester to the institute where she is scheduled for an eye operation even while scanning the papers for news of his crime. After learning the name of his victim, Diddy, impersonating a railroad official, visits the man's wife, who threatens a lawsuit, and Diddy departs, still obsessed with his crime and tormented by thoughts about death. Even when he reenacts his crime in a second visit to the tunnel, in a kind of Freudian repetition-compulsion scene, Hester refuses to see what he has done. He shouts, "I want to be seen" (289), implying that the narrative as dream is really about how unreal he feels— unacknowledged in a life that is of no consequence save for his belief that he has murdered a man and that his own death is an inescapable consequence of his actions. Ultimately, the novel seems to be posing a dilemma: Which is more real—the life that goes on day to day or the disturbed, erratic world of the human imagination? And even more perplexing is the novel's suggestion that all of the narrative has been a contrivance of a moment, the "now" that constantly recurs in the story as Diddy's life ebbs away, making the whole account the phantasmagoric tale of a dying man.

Death Kit seems a relentless effort to show how human beings, through their dreams and obsessions, have much less control over the content of their lives than they imagine. Indeed, Diddy's story, in this respect, becomes a fable about how human beings lose control of the meaning of existence. In his *Commentary* review, Theodore Solotaroff suggested that in *Death Kit,* the "unconscious is an artist—an endlessly cunning metaphysical poet."[12] The content of lives, as of works of art, is not a stable phenomenon, Sontag implies. And because content is constantly shifting in meaning, paying attention to the form—in this case of Diddy's experiences or, perhaps, dreams—is a way at least to encompass both the experience of art and of life, if not to explain them.

Many reviewers condemned *Death Kit,* and a few celebrated it. Eliot Fremont-Smith called it "tedious and insensitive to the craft of fiction." Doris Grumbach, herself a distinguished novelist, hailed Sontag's work as "a masterpiece of surrealism." Most reviewers came out somewhere in between these extremes, although few showed much enthusiasm for the novel. Richard Lehan called Sontag's work "a philosophical *tour de force,*" even while suggesting that both Diddy and the narrative remained "inchoate."[13]

The reviewers, and even later critics, did not see that *Death Kit* and *The Benefactor* were responses to Kierkegaard's book *Either/Or* (1843), a dialogic presentation of the aesthetic and ethical views of life. As Sontag put it in her diary: "*Benefactor* is a reductio ad absurdum of aesthetic approach to life— i.e. solipsistic consciousness." In *Death Kit,* reality keeps trying to break through Diddy's dreams and illusions. But neither the ethical nor the aesthetic positions were "enough," Sontag supposed. "And now? The third stage?" she queried herself.[14] She had no answer and would not present one for another twenty-five years, when she recast the aesthetic/ethical conundrum in terms of a new category: history.

In both novels, Sontag focuses on characters either determined to create their own worlds or suffer a kind of psychic break when that self-created universe cracks open. These are characters in novels that will themselves into existence just as Sontag saw her fiction as a projection of her will to create. Indeed, she vouchsafed to her diary that writing worked for her because it expressed her "autonomy," "strength,"[15] and her pride in going it alone—as she did in the positions she set out in *Styles of Radical Will.*

Sontag's second collection of essays bookends her two novels, elaborating on their themes but also bringing to a close the programmatic phase of her work. In the future, she would be less prone to stake out positions on a wide range of topics and instead would focus, in greater depth, on photography and illness, and then even more exclusively on writers' lives and works. While *Against Interpretation* and *Styles of Radical Will* were heralded as cutting-edge work, in retrospect they seem a summa of a writer who would need to change course and write a very different kind of fiction than her early essays and novels promulgated. Even that quest to become a different kind of writer, however, would be interrupted by her continuing involvement in politics, her filmmaking projects, and her desire to exert an extraliterary influence on her times.

Styles of Radical Will is divided into three parts with eight essays dealing with aesthetics, theatre and film, and politics. The lead essay, "The Aesthetics of Silence," goes beyond positions in *Against Interpretation,* exploring the uses to which modern artists have put silence as a commentary on art that fails to resolve or transcend the "painful structural contradictions inherent in the human situation" (1). And yet silence is no solution because it implies its opposite. Silence, too, in other words, has a rhetoric that may take the form of suicide, renunciation, or madness (options in Sontag's first two films and in her fiction). Silence can be as eloquent as speech—even more so in a culture surfeited with words—and can serve to focus attention and recover the power of words or to undermine them, evoking a significance that is beyond the work of art's ability to articulate. Invoking silence may also be a way for the work of art to preserve itself.

"The Aesthetics of Silence" can be read almost as a primer for *Brother Carl,* in which the eponymous main character refuses to speak. His silence can be interpreted as the artist's revulsion at a world polluted with words that merely obfuscate the agony and mystery of human existence. And yet the urge to communicate, to create art, to save the self, is an effort to overcome a silence that can lead not only to alienation but also to suicide. If silence defines the limits of speech, so speech becomes an inevitable reaction to silence, as it does in *Brother Carl,* in which Carl's friends both reveal in their words why he has retreated from the world in disgust even as their words seek to bring him back to that very same world. Silence, in other words, reveals the paradox that art can both reveal the world to us even as it also exposes art's own limitations. The political dimensions of the essay are apparent when Sontag argues that certain artists have used silence to resist the encroachment of bourgeois capitalist culture, which commodifies everything, including art. The silences in Samuel Beckett's plays, for example, concentrate the mind on the play itself, preserving its autonomy. In effect, the resort to silence is a therapeutic effort, part of the artist's spiritual project, the antidote to a materialistic culture.

Like *Against Interpretation, Styles of Radical Will* is an attack on philistines, on those who would reduce works of art to a message or theme, or demand that art observe certain moral standards. Not surprisingly, then, in

"The Pornographic Imagination" Sontag opposes the traditional rejection of pornography as lacking any purpose other than sexual fantasy, making it less than art because of its single-mindedness, lack of complexity, and inability to create rounded characters. These arguments would also exclude as art other forms of fantasy literature, melodrama, and other popular kinds of literature, Sontag suggests. She cites a number of works, such as *The Story of O* and several works by Sade to suggest that pornography, like other forms of literature, can be a critique of society. Indeed, she goes so far as to contend that pornography represents capitalism's inability to "satisfy the appetite for exalted self-transcending modes of concentration and seriousness" (68). Such comments underpin Sontag's concerted effort to undermine the power of a capitalist society to assert its authority over all forms of literature.

The subversive nature of Sontag's radicalism becomes even more apparent in the next essay, "Thinking Against Oneself: Reflections on Cioran." She praises the Romanian philosopher for his anti-systematic and yet Hegelian dialectic in which "it is the destiny of every profound idea to be quickly checkmated by another idea, which it itself has implicitly generated" (77). In Hegel, however, the dialectic leads to a synthesis, a development of history, whereas in Cioran and Sontag, the spirit of contradiction, of recanting previous views, seems a form of intellectual honesty that prevents them from codifying their thought. In her first film, *Duet for Cannibals,* Sontag tries to embody this notion of contrariety in the behavior of her characters. Thus Thomas Bauer, an aging German radical, welcomes a young disciple, Tomas, as a collaborator, encourages him to take care of Bauer's disaffected but attractive young wife, Francesca, and then turns on Tomas, accusing him of seducing Francesca and thwarting Bauer's efforts to compose his memoirs and carry on his political work. Tomas is perplexed. Bauer keeps inviting him to become more intimate, and then Bauer accuses Tomas of betraying his trust. The world, as Bauer creates it, is the artifice that human consciousness constructs, according to Cioran. And like Cioran, Bauer is in exile, a man severing his roots, and enacting Cioran's claim that we "must become metaphysically foreigners" (84).

In the second part of *Styles of Radical Will,* "Theatre and Film," the distinctions often made between stage and screen collapse, since both forms of art are artifice, no matter that theatre explores the "*continuous* use of space" (106) and film pursues the "principle of connection between" (106) images. Neither medium is more realistic than the other, and both aim for a simultaneity of effect that breaks down distinctions between genres, so that modern theatre and film play their part in demolishing the aristocratic and class-bound tastes of earlier eras.

In discussing Ingmar Bergman's *Persona*, then, Sontag resists interpreting the film as a character study, a psychological portrayal of its two female protagonists, because the director has made the distinctions between reality and illusion difficult to decipher. The film is not a story per se, Sontag insists, and not a work about psychology but about ontology and epistemology, about how we know and how we see the world. It is the confident nature of art as the representation of reality that Bergman is intent on challenging, she concludes. For Sontag, Bergman is the quintessential artist because he employs silence as a dramatization of the void, of what cannot be represented but only shown to be absent.

Similarly, Sontag's essay on Godard extols his "juxtaposition of contrary elements" (161) so that the accustomed notion that film represents reality is dislocated. Another radical, Godard unburdens himself of the cinematic conventions that his society has enforced in its effort to establish the "unified point of view" (165) expected in a film. The continuous present in his work, which seeks to abolish a sense of the past, of precedent, puts into play a deliberate rejection of the traditional search for resolution, for a story with a clear ending. Sontag sees in Godard "a provisional network of emotional and intellectual impasses" (181)—a strategy rather like that of her own films. The language of indeterminacy that Godard's films foster inform some of Sontag's own meditations in the political essays that follow.

In part three of *Styles of Radical Will*, in "Trip to Hanoi," Sontag confesses that she found it difficult to embed her "evolving radical political convictions" (203) into her earlier prose because she studiously avoided an autobiographical approach. However, in her visit to North Vietnam she confronts a range of factors: her own reasons for the journey (to express her opposition to the war), her relationships with her fellow travelers (also war protestors), the disorienting impact of measuring her Western sensibility against that of the North Vietnamese, and her disconcerting realization that she is being treated like a movie star. Although in basic sympathy with the North Vietnamese, whom she sees as fighting for their independence and fending off an aggressive American attack, she has trouble adjusting to Vietnamese groupthink and is compelled to explain why she judges the North Vietnamese by a different standard—different, that is, from the one she applies to her own government.

Sontag's discomfort arises from her admitted ignorance. Thrust into an alien culture, she cannot be certain of her judgments. Unlike Cuban revolutionaries, who were passionate and informal, the North Vietnamese seem stolid and hierarchical. In general, though, she strives to overcome her reservations about what she sees and is relieved to find that the North Vietnamese do not suffer from the "complex kind of pessimism" (245) that she associates with Westerners. Although they seem depersonalized and even dehumanized in some respects, she admires their courage and solidarity, which she regards as a passionate form of patriotism.

A good deal of what Sontag seeks in North Vietnam is a result of her anger over American culture and the policies of the American government. In "What's Happening in America," the piece that precedes "Trip to Hanoi," she excoriates the United States as a country founded on genocide. What is more, she ties the depredation of the North American continent with a wave of immigrants ignorant of culture and eager to subdue native peoples and minorities in the quest to develop a crude and materialistic society. She calls American leaders "yahoos" (196, 264), thus linking them to the philistines she deplores in her literary essays. For her, only the radicalism of a new generation can hope to reverse the cancerous legacy of "Western Faustian" (201) man.

Critics understood that Sontag was attempting to make a "radical connection between esthetics and politics," as John Leonard put it.[16] Many of them dismissed her effort, as he did colorfully, by calling her a "deracinated urban griefchik." Others, like Christopher Lehmann-Haupt, were aghast at her simplistic political judgments and overgeneralizations, especially her comment that the white race was the "cancer of human history"—a comment that seemed unworthy of a writer with such an otherwise impressive critical mind.[17] To be sure, other reviewers, such as John Weightman, were impressed with *Styles of Radical Will,* especially with the opening section, and Jonathan Raban extolled the breadth of her writing, comparing it to Emerson's "casserole style of essay writing."[18]

Sontag herself regarded "The Aesthetics of Silence," for example, as an advance on her work in *Against Interpretation.* She emphasized to interviewer Edwin Newman that she had been exploring the limitations of art from the point of view of the artists themselves, and not their critics.[19] She might have extended that observation to suggest that "Trip to Hanoi" was an effort to critique herself and the limitations of her own Western, aesthetic sensibility as it encountered an alien culture. It would take, however, more than another decade for her to come to terms with the weaknesses in her political writing, and it would take even longer for her to propose a reading of history that superseded the faults of her earlier work.

CHAPTER 3

Photography and Film

Although *On Photography* was not published until 1977, it emanated from a series of essays Sontag began writing in the early 1970s—work that would be interrupted by her breast cancer, which would take nearly three years to treat, and by an uncertainty about how to proceed as a writer after her first four books seemed to define her as a critic and theorist rather than as the novelist she aspired to be. Her diary from this period reflects a writer discouraged by the reception of both her films and her novels, although she was full of ideas for both, and achieved considerable critical success with a documentary, *Promised Lands* (1974).

Shot in Israel after the Yom Kippur War, Sontag's film is an exploration of Jewish identity—including her own, as she freely admitted to interviewers. Arabs have no voice in the film; that is, none are interviewed, although the sounds and images of Arabs are everywhere in this probing study of the land and the Jewish and Arab claims to it. The film is also an exemplification of her writing about photography, a problematic form of recording and interpreting the world. On the one hand, Sontag noted that photographs seem so real that they are used as documentary evidence. On the other hand, like all representations of reality, photographs distort and are subject to all sorts of distortions, depending on how they are cropped, edited, lit, angled, and presented (with or without captions). Thus *Promised Lands* is a work of art that comments not only on its ostensible subject matter but on itself. As Howard Kissel noted, Sontag let the "images speak for themselves" even as she recognized that they, too, were subject to criticism since the images could be paradoxical, contradictory, and ambiguous.[1] Again and again the film is framed with commentary, which is itself framed by shots of the land and people the commentators discuss. No closure, no final interpretation of what the film means is possible because of its

Hegelian methodology, which, as Stanley Kauffmann noted, exposes the partiality of truth that the images and the monologues explore.[2] Although some reviewers disparaged *Promised Lands* as "haphazard," to use Nora Sayre's word, and called the film "stupefyingly tedious" (David Moran), Byron Stuart spoke for many others in observing the sharp contrast between the abstractions of Sontag's on-camera witnesses and the concrete reality of the film's images. And previous denigrators of Sontag's work, such as the critic John Simon, gave the film a respectful reception.[3]

More than Sontag's early novels and two previous films, *Promised Lands* is able to reify her persistent desire to investigate the world of dreams (illusions) and how those conceptions or abstractions impinge on reality, a reality that the camera can make more palpable than Sontag's prose. But in a way *Promised Lands* also questions the viability of documentary itself, of its effectiveness in presenting a complex vision of reality and individual perceptions of that reality. Photographs, as Sontag argues in *On Photography*, are subject to all the limitations that beset any form of interpretation. As a result, the only way forward is to constantly question what photographs show, what commentators say, and to create, as she does in *On Photography*, an anthology of all that has been said about photography as a medium of communication. John Simon described Sontag's vision in *Promised Lands* as "tragic irony," perfectly capturing her contention that a double perspective is needed—which, again, is a Hegelian approach revealing that an idea, when pushed to its extreme, turns into its opposite, which, in turn, is the very definition of irony.

That Sontag began her work as a series of essays before conceiving of them as a book is important in assessing the style and structure of *On Photography*. Each essay was a process of discovery for her, and given her adversarial attitude toward her own writing—her desire to argue with herself—each essay also becomes a response and even a counterargument to the previous one. Furthermore, for book publication she extensively revised and expanded the essays. As a result, *On Photography* is her most layered and textured work, reflecting the back-and-forth of thinking about a subject that is never quite settled in her mind and, indeed, became a subject to which she would return in *Regarding the Pain of Others*.

"In Plato's Cave," the first essay, provides the gist of an argument that she continues to refine, augment, adjust, and correct in subsequent essays and, in fact, throughout her career. In this opening gambit, she takes issue with the common tendency to regard photographs as not merely statements about the world but as "pieces of it" (4). In fact, at best photographs are fragments of reality—but not even that, to be precise—because they are reflections of the world, not the world itself. They are, in sum, like those images reflected on the cave walls of Plato's allegory about truth. We cannot see the truth directly; we only apprehend it indirectly as the images or shadows cast by the truth. Truth cannot exist in and of itself, in other words, but must be interpreted. In this respect, photographs are no different from any other representation of truth: photographs do not speak for themselves any more than facts speak for themselves, even though it has often been said that they do. And because photographs are fragments, they make of the world a piecework of items (photographs) that are reductive because they represent only a part of the world. Even more problematic is the phenomenon of packaging photographs, for then they too become artifacts, objects in themselves that are part of a photographer's design. In short, photographs impose themselves on the world and appropriate the world, making it impossible to view photographs as more innocent and less meddling with reality than other kinds of art.

Even more disturbing, photography is a kind of imperialistic enterprise, taking possession of the world and making of the world an opportunity to produce more photographs, and not necessarily more truth. The hegemony of the photograph, even in the hands of tourists, is another way in which the world's complexity is diminished. Indeed, what gets into photographs is what is photogenic, which means that certain aspects of the world are obscured or ignored. The significance of all events and places are shaped in terms of the medium of photography.

An almost sinister aspect of photography becomes apparent when Sontag suggests that it can be used as a weapon to shoot the world. Photographers go gunning for images and saturate human consciousness with visuals that actually disconnect viewers from reality. Photographs destroy narrative and a sense of continuity and temporality. History, the complex developments of time, is subsumed in the spatial frame of the photograph. What results is not knowledge but its semblance, which can be an arresting, even erotic, attraction to images without the requisite intellectual grasp of what those images purport to show.

Sontag's relentless exposure of photography's limitations resulted in considerable opposition to her arguments, with many critics pointing out how photographs contribute to an understanding of the world. However, as Sontag pointed out in her diaries, she was a polemical writer. She began by staking out a position and exploring its implications. In other words, she would not let go of an argument until she had exhausted its power. She was quite willing to return to the same argument later, as she did in *Regarding the Pain of Others,* and modify or even reject the premises of earlier arguments, replacing them with antithetical interpretations. But in the full heat of her first essay on photography, she felt obliged to continue the momentum of what almost could be called

"Against Photography." That she did not give the book such a title reflects, as she freely admitted, her own attraction to photographs, which is why she begins with Plato, for Sontag includes herself in the masses who have been seduced by photographs and taken them for truth.

In "America Seen Through Photographs, Darkly," Sontag suggests that photography has become an extension of Walt Whitman's ambition to make a democratic art of poetry, and to make art itself a demystifying organ of perception. Anything, in the age of Andy Warhol, can be pictured or photographed as art. As the essay's title implies, Sontag is skeptical of this kind of democratization because it blends everything together and makes everything equally important, as in Edward Steichen's 1955 "Family of Man" exhibition at the Museum of Modern Art. This quest to universalize experience, to make all peoples one and the same, destroys a sense of history and makes politics irrelevant. Opposed to this Whitmanian tradition is photographer Diane Arbus, whose photographs insist on the specificity, even the alienness, of her human subjects. They have been called "freaks," Sontag notes. Even so, Arbus cannot escape the reductive and misleading nature of her medium, so that her portraits, shot straight on, create the illusion of self-revelation, as if her subjects remain part of Whitman's project to fully disclose his nation through his art. The freaks, then, become just part of the democratic mix.

Focusing on Arbus's biography, Sontag wonders whether the photographs of freaks actually diminished the photographer's sense of pain that led to her suicide. Has Arbus done no more than simply expand the range of acceptable subjects in photographs rather than reveal anything of significance about them? Sontag compares the Jewish Arbus to Jewish writer Nathanael West in presenting "deformed and mutilated" (42) subjects in reaction to family values and culture that promoted healthy mindedness. Were Arbus's photographs a reaction against the glossy commercial world she had worked in, treating that world with an irony that is absent from the work of Andy Warhol, another artist who began in commercial art? Sontag sees Arbus's work, whatever its limitations, as a rebuke to Whitman's belief that he could comprehend the whole country through his art.

At this stage of her argument, in "Melancholy Objects," Sontag is ready to take on the putative realism of photographs, contending that they are actually a species of surrealism. By putting up borders around reality with its images, photography is inherently surrealistic, reshaping and bending the world to its medium, which is superficial, a reading of surfaces without depth. She notes that certain photographers have nevertheless thought of themselves as scientists or moralists, romantics, and documentarians, but what their work gains in explanatory power, it also loses in its selectiveness, class bias, or refusal to make distinctions in subject matter so that everything is simultaneously important but as a result also unimportant. Photographs injure time, scrambling moral and historical differences, which certain photographs attempt to remedy by the use of captions and commentary. These editorial attachments to photographs she compares to critic Walter Benjamin's use of quotations as a way of collecting the world.

"The Heroism of Vision" continues Sontag's exploration of photography's superficiality, its attraction to surfaces as opposed to paintings, for example, which are constructions and reveal more than the moment photographs disclose. To see is not to know, she points out, and yet the modern sensibility has become enamored of the lens as a way of identifying reality. Knowledge and pleasure become an ocular phenomenon—so much so that the ethical and contextual nature of truth is overwhelmed by the seeming concreteness and specificity of photographs. And the sheer quantity of photographs makes it impossible to determine what is truly significant and truthful. As the essay's title suggests, the photographic way of seeing has been valorized to the detriment of other ways of knowing.

"Photographic Evangels" centers on the contradictory arguments of photographers, which seems to Sontag defensive. Is photography the product of rational choices the artist makes, or is it a fluid, intuitive medium, expressive of a spontaneity other arts cannot rival? Is the photograph a record or the product of a personal, aesthetic vision? The questions arise because photographers have given such varying, conflicting answers. She suggests that the medium is "inherently equivocal" (123), which is one reason why she hesitates to call it art. Compared to the fine arts, especially painting, photography can seem undiscriminating, "promiscuous" (129).[4] And this is why photographers have had to argue so strenuously for the aesthetic nature of their enterprise. Part of the problem as well is the extensive vocabulary that has been developed for evaluating paintings and the still meager language used to describe photographs. Too often the photograph is merely called "interesting" (138).

"The Image-World," Sontag's final essay, comes full circle to her beginning invocation of Plato. Given the infinite reproducibility of photographs, what does it mean to call one photograph an original and another a copy? Such distinctions have always been important in fine art, but the duplication of photographs calls into questions its status as art—at least in traditional terms. Judging photography by the highest standards is also complicated by the developments in technology that have made cameras so user-friendly and portable. Can anyone be an artist? An artist by accident? Can photographs be an aid to reflection, or do photographs deflect the ability to analyze reality. How, in sum, can photographs be curated, singled out, and deemed art? Somehow, Sontag suggests, an ecology of images has to be established.

As a way of displaying the manifold ways photography has been described, analyzed, and promoted, the book includes "A Brief Anthology of Quotations." This section might be thought of as Sontag's own ecological response to photography, since she selects those statements that highlight the possibilities and limitation of the photographical medium.

It is hardly surprising that given the power of Sontag's polemical book, and the publicity given to her ideas, that many reviewers took issue with her vision of photography. Ben Lifson criticized Sontag for not acknowledging the pleasures of photography and of not doing justice to its ethical and aesthetic possibilities. In effect, she was as reductive about photography as she said photography was about reality. Edward Grossman called *On Photography* a "profoundly reactionary meditation" by a bookish person who preferred words over images. Candace Leonard contended that Sontag could not speak of "reality" without an intervening medium such as photography. All reality had to be contextualized or framed in some way. Alfred Kazin pointed out that language could distort reality as much as photography and like other critics was uneasy about Sontag's penchant for separating photography from the social and historical context in which it emerged. Similarly, Harvey Green wondered why photographs should be any more distorting than documents. Weren't both fragments? In fact, this weakness in *On Photography* was what Sontag set out to remedy later in *Regarding the Pain of Others*. Laurie Stone deplored Sontag's analogies: "If comparing cancer to an imperialist army distorts our concept of cancer, doesn't comparing a camera to a gun distort the reality of a camera?" Even Sontag's anthology of quotations came in for criticism. Paul Lewis argued that she had engaged in a surrealism that was like the very photography she attacked.[5]

While *On Photography* received mostly mixed to negative reviews, several distinguished critics seemed more attuned to her tone and manner. William Gass, for example, described *On Photography* as "brief but brilliant," a "meditation, not a treatise," which is to say that the book was not as doctrinaire as several reviewers made it out to be. In like fashion Michael Starenko appreciated Sontag's dialectical approach, which revealed a process of thinking about photography that he found extraordinarily valuable. Rudolf Arnheim extolled Sontag's "rhapsodic" style," and if John Simon was not certain what to make of Sontag's own position on photography, he admired her for presenting "unanswered questions in the place of false security and dangerous misconceptions." Robert Melville was less troubled by knowing exactly where Sontag stood, regarding the book as a whole, including her anthology of quotations, as indicative of her "ironic neutrality."[6]

Sontag herself responded to the reviews by calling out critics on her use of the word "aggressive." In itself, she told interviewer Jonathan Cott, "aggressive" was true of almost any form of activity, any assertion of self in the world. Sontag herself loved photographs, she insisted, and perhaps attending more to that aspect of her experience might have quelled some of the criticism. At any rate, she also took a much broader view of her work than did the reviewers. She suggested that *On Photography* was part of her quest to "ask what it means to be modern."[7]

Sontag's near final words on the subject of photography come in *Regarding the Pain of Others* (2003). Here she begins by analyzing Virginia Woolf's response to photographs of atrocities during the Spanish Civil War. Woolf, a pacifist, argued in *Three Guineas,* that the slaughter of noncombatants depicted in the photographs aroused the deepest rejection of war. But to Sontag, the photographs might also cause others to increase support for the besieged Spanish republic. Woolf's reading of the photographs denied the possibility of a political reaction informed by knowledge of Spain's history. This judgment, undoubtedly informed by Sontag's own experiences in the siege of Sarajevo, also signals how much she had changed as a writer, who now included in her nonfiction and fiction a profound awareness of history and how it shapes our perceptions.

She also brought to *Regarding the Pain of Others* a much more acute understanding of how much human psychology and politics can sensitize or desensitize reactions to photographs. It had become standard practice to dismiss photographs as fabricated if they did not support one's politics (10). What is more, the same photograph can result in contrary responses: "A call for peace. A cry for revenge" (13). And a more neutral observer may just take atrocity photographs as further confirmation of a terrible world. Consequently, it is far more difficult to pin down the implications of a photograph. Readers of the Kindle edition of *Regarding the Pain of Others* have highlighted this passage: "In contrast to a written account—which, depending on its complexity of thought, reference, and vocabulary, is pitched at a larger or smaller readership —a photograph has only one language and is destined potentially for all" (20).[8] Even more Kindle readers have been taken with Sontag's questioning of Woolf's assertion that "Photographs are not an argument; they are simply a crude statement of fact addressed to the eye" (26). To this Sontag rejoins that photographs cannot be regarded simply as evidence, as facts, and given their status also as personal testimony, she questions how can they be regarded as an "objective record" (26).[9] The photographer's intentions, Sontag adds, cannot determine the photograph's significance, since it will be taken up and distorted by many different viewers for their own purposes (39).

Much more than in *On Photography,* Sontag explores in *Regarding the Pain of Others* the way photographs actually enter the world, which is often as "staged" or composed—like other works of art. Photographs are associated with real moments, and yet, as with the raising of the flag at Iwo Jima, such "real" moments have been reenacted for the camera. And because photographs seem so much a part of the world they represent, it comes as a shock and a disappointment when we learn that so-called reality has been composed or re-composed. The idea of performing for the camera, as Theodore Roosevelt did when he agreed to retake San Juan Hill one more time so that it would look more exciting, disabuses the viewer of the notion that photographs can ever be, as Woolf said, "a crude statement of fact." They are often not crude at all but practiced and polished. Thus, to this day, Robert Capa's photograph of a soldier falling in the moment of death has been challenged. Did the death really occur in war, and was Capa's work fortuitous? Was the photograph taken during a military exercise? Evidence exists to support the truth of what Capa shot, but the issue, Sontag suggests, cannot be settled because of photography's ambiguous status as both faithful report and interpretation.

Sontag also confronts the question of what ultimate impact photographs have. Is there a time limit on shocked reactions to gruesome photographs of war? Doesn't shock wear off as the viewer becomes inured to what is seen? And yet Sontag contends that "habituation is not automatic" (82). On the contrary, outrage and shock can also increase with repeated viewings. Just as paintings of the crucifixion do not become jejune for the faithful, so photographs of atrocities can continue to appall and provoke a full-hearted response. Indeed, the power of certain pictures may be so great that people look away from them, which is a way of saying their impact has not abated.

Still, as in *On Photography,* Sontag is troubled by the limitations of photography when compared to narrative. Photographs cannot present arguments or stories. She takes issue, for example, with *New York Times* correspondent John Kifner, who claimed of one war photograph that "the image is stark, one of the most enduring of the Balkan wars: a Serb militiaman casually kicking a dying Muslim woman in the head. It tells you everything you need to know" (89). Not so, Sontag protests. She then dates the photograph (April 1992), taken during the first month of the Serbian "rampage through Bosnia" (90). Even though the photograph is quite detailed, as Sontag describes it, she suggests that the "photograph tells us very little—except that war is hell, and that graceful young men with guns are capable of kicking overweight older women lying helpless, or already killed, in the head" (90). Don't such photographs, and others taken during the Vietnam War, serve to "confirm what we already know (or want to know)?" (92), Sontag asks. It is a genuine question—like several she poses about the need to observe and for some to protest the grisly and barbaric rites of war.

Sontag is more certain that even seemingly apathetic responses to photographs of war atrocities are the reactions of those who may be "full of feelings; the feelings are rage and frustration" (125). *Regarding the Pain of Others* expresses her "irresistible temptation" (104) to quarrel with the premise of *On Photography*—that "in a world saturated, no, hyper-saturated with images, those that should matter have a diminishing effect; we become callous" (105). She wonders what evidence there is to support the notion that "our culture of spectatorship neutralized the moral force of photographs of atrocities" (105)? And her own solution, calling for an "ecology of images"—in sum, for a more discriminating response to photography—is impossible. There can be no committee, no guardians, to "ration horror, to keep fresh its ability to shock" (106).

Sontag now identifies a reality that "exists independent of the attempts to weaken its authority" (109) through photographs, which frame and also leave out vital details. Photographs do fragment the world, Sontag still believes, but the world itself, history, remains whole. In other words, we do not view the world exclusively through media like television. Indeed, she dismisses the arguments for a world that is now moderated, so to speak, by media as "fancy rhetoric." She specifically attacks French thinkers such as Guy Debord and Jean Baudrillard who believe images have become reality. She calls their argument "something of a French specialty" (109). It is their kind of thinking about the "death of reality" that led to the idea that the siege of Sarajevo would be stopped or not depending on how the media covered it. Sontag, who put her life on the line in several visits to the shelled city, where trips out into the street exposed her to sniper fire, believes she was in touch with a reality that could not be entirely captured or defined by the camera. "To speak of reality becoming a spectacle is a breathtaking provincialism," she contends. "It universalizes the viewing habits of a small, educated population living in the rich part of the world, where news has been converted into entertainment" (110). But the world contains real suffering, and its consequences cannot be obliterated by "those zones in the well-off countries where people have the dubious privilege of being spectators, or of declining to be spectators, of other people's pain, just as it is absurd to generalize about the ability to respond to the sufferings of others on the basis of the mind-set of those consumers of news who know nothing at first hand about war and massive injustice and terror. There are hundreds of millions of television watchers who are far from inured to what they see on television. They do not have the luxury of patronizing reality" (109).

Drawing on her own trips to Sarajevo, and mindful of those who attacked her as a grandstanding visitor, Sontag launches her defense by arguing against jaded intellectuals who are incapable of experiencing the reality of war. These modern thinkers see the violence as a spectacle and therefore see her own participation in the siege as insincere. She suggests that some commentators do all that is possible to prevent themselves from being engaged in the suffering of others. Instead, they sit back, confident of their superiority and liken her to photographers who are "war tourists" (111). The role of those photographers and their photographs, she emphasizes, is to ask us to "pay attention, to reflect, to learn, to examine the rationalization for mass suffering offered by established powers. Who caused what the picture shows? Who is responsible? Is it excusable? Was it inevitable?" (117). It is no refutation of these photographs to note that some people will not look at them or will change the channel.

The argument that impugns photographs because they are just a form of watching also provokes Sontag's rebuke. Photographs are just another way of watching the world—not the only way. Like the mind itself, photographs both view and stand back from the world itself, and "there's nothing wrong with standing back and thinking" (118), Sontag affirms. In the end, she contends that there is no substitute for experiencing war or any kind of reality firsthand. But photographs, like other reports about the world, express the need to draw as close as possible even if we cannot be right there. For those who are there, Sontag concedes ultimate authority. We cannot understand, and cannot imagine. But underpinning her argument is also an unspoken rebuttal: we certainly need to try.

Like *On Photography*, *Regarding the Pain of Others* received mixed reviews, with critics once again spoiling to take issue with Sontag—as did Peter Conrad, who asserted that photographs were not any more influential or powerful than words. Revolutionary slogans did quite as well as photographs before the camera was invented, he pointed out. So, how could words be the "antidote to images"? Conrad noted that the book was an amplification of a Sontag lecture and as such seemed bloated and repetitive. John Leonard, who had closely followed Sontag's career, saw her as still "shuffling contradictions" and "dealing provocations." He seemed less impressed with her individual arguments than with her continuing ability to "make us think." And this was the response of other reviewers who were willing to honor the gravity of Sontag's arguments, even if they were not certain that she was right. As a later critic, Philip Lopate, puts it in his book *Notes on Sontag*, *Regarding the Pain of Others* is "altogether a more measured, sober, qualifying and open-ended book" (190) than *On Photography*.[10]

Lopate also notes that the prose style of the later book is "less preening . . . and inclined to break into sentence fragments: 'Photographs of atrocities may give rise to opposing responses. A call for peace. A cry for revenge. Or simply the bemused awareness, continually restocked by photographic information, that terrible things happen.' This is the prose manner of late Sontag: forthright, conversational, much-interviewed, and hearing that interviewee voice in her head, transcribing it straight out" (190). Yet she is still prone to overstatement, Lopate suggests, qualifying his own praise. She seems unduly sure that certain wartime photographs have been staged when the evidence is not altogether clear. Lopate senses that for all Sontag's willingness to recant some of her opinions about photography, she is still a profound skeptic of the optics of photographs—that by seeing we can also know what is seen.

Although released two decades before *Regarding the Pain of Others* and five years after the publication of *On Photography,* Sontag's film *Unguided Tour* (1982) seems like a coda to her studies of the visual image. Set in Venice, the film includes the customary shots of St. Mark's Cathedral, the canals, the palaces, the leonine faces on the facades of bridges and buildings, but set against these monuments is the troubled tour a couple makes of the city state. Their mood seems taken from the Sontag story with the same title (included in *I, etcetera*), and from a single sentence: "They say a trip is a good time for repairing a damaged love" (e-book location 2930). Lucinda Childs, Sontag's lover when the film was shot, is the film's austere and elegant heroine, a dancer who walks with a studied grace as her male companion follows her lead, trying to sort out her moods with imploring and yearning looks that are reminiscent of Sontag's own plangent passages of lovesickness in her diaries. Childs was an exquisite choice to exemplify the lover as an object of veneration. The camera lingers on her taut somber profile, her lean and supple body, her dark and brooding brows, her withholding gestures, as she turns away from her lover's attempt to kiss her. Later in a courtyard solo, she turns her body into a pinwheel in imitation of the pinwheels that are shown spinning together in several shots. The dance encompasses her aloof attractiveness and the whirling emotions that she prefers to contain within herself.

The scene constantly shifts from streets, to squares, to boats, to canals, to a palace interior where it seems, momentarily, that the couple have reconciled, merging together in a wonderful waltzing routine. But this reunion is fleeting as the couple is parted once again in the estrangement of their separate selves. Tourism is no way to begin again; it is, in fact, as the story "Unguided Tour" suggests, a way of ending things. Seeing the world as a spectacle, as a picture, as a photograph, is a romantic quest but also an evasion of reality, of the waters that are slowly rising in the Venice of *Unguided Tour*. Everyone becomes awash with an encroaching grim reality that neither the buildings nor the people pictured gazing and grouping around these edifices can assuage or ameliorate. Sontag's equation of photographs with an evasion of reality perhaps accounts for her diary entry for February 21, 1977: Sontag included "being photographed" and "taking photographs" (416) in her list of things she disliked.

And yet Sontag's interest in photographs and photographers never waned. Indeed, as her lover Annie Leibovitz reports in *A Photographer's Life,* Sontag encouraged Leibovitz to always have a camera on hand—even when she was off duty, so to speak. Sontag became one of Leibovitz's favorite subjects, and Sontag contributed an introduction to Leibovitz's collection *Women* (1999), reprinted in *Where the Stress Falls*. The book is a sampling, Sontag suggests, of how women's roles have changed in the past decade, although she regards them still as a minority in every sense except the numerical. Thus, Sontag writes, Leibovitz photographs women engaging in "new zones of achievement" (237), even as they remain subject to degrading stereotypes. Women are a unique subject, Sontag argues, a work in progress in a way that men are not. By simply appearing in these photographs, women are modeling examples of success, self-esteem, victimhood, and aging well. Women are shown in roles that men have already made their own, and so they become objects of interrogation that would not arouse interest in a book devoted to men. She notes that restrictive views of women are embedded in language—all languages that never use the pronoun "she" to refer to humanity as a whole.

In the history of photography, women are most often portrayed for their beauty and men for their character: "Men didn't look wistful. Women, ideally, didn't look forceful" (240), Sontag notes. Even when women became photographers, such as Julia Margaret Cameron, they adopted the male view of women. Cameron photographed "exalted" portraits of femininity. So ingrained is the subject of women as beauties that a collection of photographs without beautiful women in it might well be regarded as misogynistic, Sontag suggests. The only exception she allows in her catalogue of women as beautiful types, existing to be photographed for their beauty of form, is the depiction of goddesses and other mythic creatures, but such women are the subjects of sculpture and painting, not photography, which most often situated women in the domestic sphere.

In the new economic reality of America, women must work, and that fact alone has changed the way women are viewed and the way they view themselves, Sontag observes. Feminism may have helped changed attitudes toward women, but the way they make a living has made the decisive break with traditional definitions of womanhood. Even so, emphasizing the feminine in photographs of powerful women still seems a requirement, Sontag insists. And it is still regarded as a virtue for a woman to subordinate herself to her husband, as in the famous line from *A Star is Born,* when Vicki Lester (Judy Garland in the 1954 version) announces to the audience, "This is Mrs. Norman Main," in tribute to the husband who discovered her and helped make her a star.

In Leibovitz's photographs, Sontag sees women for the first time emerging as themselves, doing their jobs, and not catering to the convention of how attractive women are supposed to be posed for the camera. Even better, in *Women,* there is a "plurality of models" (248). The lack of a prescriptive program for women obviously delights Sontag. Eschewing any specific commentary on the photographs, Sontag wants the book to remain "open-ended." And she closes her essay with the same statement followed by a question that undermines the statement: "A photograph is not an opinion. Or is it?" (249).

In one of the most searching reviews of *Women,* Peter M. Stevenson identified the problem with Sontag's apparent unwillingness to interpret Leibovitz's photographs except in the most general sense:

> Ms. Leibovitz ends her acknowledgments with, "I am extremely grateful to Anna Wintour and *Vogue.*" If only Ms. Sontag had written an essay that tackled head-on Ms. Leibovitz's financial and artistic symbiosis with "today's hugely complex fashion-and-photography system." What would she make of the photograph, taken from below, of the red panties and crotches of four faceless, high-kicking Kilgore College Rangerette cheerleaders? Is it commentary—the male sports establishment exploits women by making them dress up as cheerleaders—or is it appreciation? How does the photograph jibe with Ms. Sontag's statement that this is a book about women's "ambition," which women have been "schooled to stifle in themselves"? Is a photograph of women's underwear a celebration of ambition?

Stevenson is perhaps not quite fair, since Sontag does say that some of the photographs show that women have not made much progress. A more specific criticism might ask, *Which photographs are which?* And that is perhaps Stephenson's point. There is such a thing as being too open-ended.[11]

In her studies of photography Sontag has often contextualized her interpretations of photographs by dealing with the biographies—or at least with the careers—of photographers. That she does not do so with Leibovitz provokes an unanswered question. Was Sontag's personal connection to the photographer perhaps a factor in her decision not to analyze the photographs? To have done so would have been to tie Leibovitz to her own cultural moment and her implication in both the commercial and aesthetic aspects of photography to which Stevenson alludes in his review.

CHAPTER 4

Illness and Its Metaphors

Although in interviews Susan Sontag spoke openly about her cancer diagnosis, including the dire prediction that she had only a 10 percent chance of surviving much beyond the course of her treatment, *Illness as Metaphor* never mentions her own case. She believed that references to her own experience actually undermined her authority. She did not want her ideas about disease to be infected, so to speak, with her personal testimony. She wanted her arguments to stand on their own, and to have her voice be taken as a conduit for important insights, not as a voice that had some special claim on readers because of her own personality or background. She rejected the romantic notion that writing is self-expression. She wrote to create literature and a body of ideas and not to convey some conception of herself. She was at the service of the written word. She wrote to discover insights, not to disseminate perceptions she already had formulated before composing her sentences.

Sontag's attitude toward literature carried over to her reactions to illness. She did not regard cancer as an expression of certain personalities, which is to say no one could cause his or her own disease. Cancer was not the product of a psychological problem, such as repression. Holding in your feelings did not give you cancer. And yet, as she demonstrates in *Illness as Metaphor*, the history of writing about disease reflects precisely this tendency to attribute tuberculosis, for example, to a certain kind of passionate and febrile sensitivity that made poets, for example, susceptible to what was once called "consumption," connected to certain emotions that were eating up the writer's body. On the contrary, argues Sontag in *Illness as Metaphor*, diseases such as tuberculosis and cancer have to do with the chemistry of the body, with cells gone awry, not with a certain kind of sensibility. The body, in other words, is a vehicle for the disease, but the disease does not emanate from the behavior of its victim. Illness is not a romantic phenomenon; people do not make themselves sick, even though that common expression greatly influences so many discussions of disease and makes patients blame themselves for their maladies.

Sontag begins her book by evoking the very idea of illness as a disrupting experience that severs the afflicted from their everyday lives. Thus she universalizes her subject. Everyone has been sick, and illness is a more encompassing word than disease. But her point is that disease must be regarded no differently from any other illness. Disease has a physical cause, and to dramatize or poeticize it by the use of metaphors means that the origins of sickness are obscured and distorted. Illness becomes something other than itself and, in the case of certain diseases such as cancer or tuberculosis, a mystique is engendered that can prevent patients from seeking ways to alleviate or cure their suffering and can also dissuade doctors from delivering the diagnoses of certain diseases for fear that their alarmed patients will not be able to cope with their affliction. Metaphorical thinking about illness, in short, must be resisted, even though the inclination to think in terms of metaphors is powerful.

As in all of her work, Sontag resists the tendency to psychologize—in this case, to view cancer as a disease different from others, as some kind of sickness of the psyche, a shameful affliction that has to be hidden. To view illness this way is to moralize, to stigmatize the sufferer as somehow to blame. When Sontag was writing her book in the mid-1970s, it was still common practice for doctors to withhold from patients the knowledge that they had cancer. It was like a dirty secret or, at best, a mystery like tuberculosis in the nineteenth century—before it was understood that the disease was spread by a bacillus.

Each disease has its own set of associations—tuberculosis with the wasting of the body but also with passion. The tubercular patient, fevered and flushed, can be imagined as sexually desirable whereas cancer is regarded as depriving the body of sexual allure. Whereas tuberculosis is connected with the lungs and the breath of life, cancer is a frightening, internal, invisible attacker, although in fact, as Sontag points out, tuberculosis can strike other parts of the body. In other words, the mythology of the disease obscures and distorts its nature and its location. Cancer, on the other hand, can appear virtually anywhere in the body and is, therefore, like the appearance of death itself.

Tuberculosis leading to hemorrhages is an expressive disease, long attached to ideas of a passion frustrated (as in the case of Keats's longing for Fanny Brawne), whereas cancer is attributed to persons who have sublimated their desires, resulting in a will that is throttled and blocked, a body and mind that turns in upon itself, causing sickness. In the nineteenth century, the tubercular sufferer could be romanticized as a spirit divesting itself of its corporeal, corruptible self, a soul too sensitive for this world. A cancer sufferer, on the other

hand, did not fit the romantic tropes. Cancer seemed a disease that only isolated the self, with none of the appealing characteristics that formed the mythology of the consumptive. Only in 1944, when streptomycin, an antibiotic, was
discovered to cure tuberculosis, did the disease's mythology give way to the
scientific etiology of the illness.

To a great extent, Sontag's attack on the mythologizing of disease is also an
attack on the romantic sensibility in which cancer can have no place of honor
because it is not seen as a positive expression of human will but just the reverse:
a fatalistic relinquishment of action. Cancer is thus regarded as a defeat of the
human spirit, an antiheroic illness that demeans the sufferer and deprives the
self of its own striving to succeed. The consequences of such thinking are dire,
Sontag argues, since cancer patients with such defeatist attitudes will not seek
aggressive forms of treatment, or indeed any proper treatment since they regard cancer as a death sentence. Although this negative attitude toward cancer
has abated—thanks in part to Sontag's efforts to expose the fallacy of such de-
moralizing behavior—the remnants of this fatalism remain in those who speak
of conquering cancer, or of a war on cancer, as if cancer is not just a disease but
a kind of evil force inside the self that must be resisted. When Sontag writes,
then, of proper treatment she is suggesting a rational, calm response devoid of
metaphors that characterize the disease but do nothing to show how it might
be alleviated and even cured.

To resort to psychological explanations, Sontag reiterates, is to subvert the
reality of illness. If one is a victim of one's own personality, she points out, then
the effort to overcome the disease is futile. In this way, the individual sufferer
fails to take responsibility for dealing with his or her sickness. Cancer then
becomes a self-punishing disease that is also ratified by society at large when
the disease is not acknowledged forthrightly. This kind of fanciful and puni-
tive thinking about cancer became in the Victorian age the notion that cancer
stemmed from low energy, just as in her own time Wilhelm Reich contended
that the disease resulted from "unexpressed energy." Even more deleterious, in
Sontag's view, is the paranoia that a cancer diagnosis engenders, so that the
proliferating cancer cells become alien invaders, taking over the body as in science fiction.

As Sontag notes in her book, however, the understanding of cancer, and
of many different kinds of cancers, began to disrupt the cancer narrative,
although the dread the disease can still provoke should not be minimized.
Nevertheless, her prediction that the language used to describe cancer and its
forms of treatment would change as more about the manifold nature of the disease is revealed has been confirmed—even if the very metaphors she deplored,

especially the calls for a "war on cancer," continue to prevail. Indeed, no obituary of a cancer death can be complete without some mention of the way the disease was battled. Hence *Illness as Metaphor* retains its relevance and brilliance, challenging readers to think carefully about the words they use and the extent to which those words accurately describe or distort the nature of illness.

Both the range and quantity of comment on *Illness as Metaphor* makes this Sontag's most widely read and influential book. As usual, some commentators wished to quarrel with her approach, her arguments, and her examples. William Logan deplored Sontag's lack of historical grounding and dismissed her argument as too literary. Similarly, Maggie Scarf thought Sontag made too much of the metaphorical description of disease and thought that responses to cancer should be regarded more generally as part of the response to mortality. Dennis Donoghue was even more dismissive, charging that the book lacked evidence that it tried to overcome with heated rhetoric. A. Alvarez concurred, terming Sontag's arguments "curiously brutal."[1]

But the overwhelmingly positive response overrode the mixed reviews. John Leonard praised Sontag's "creative binge" and for writing a book unmarred by the "mannerism and glibness" of earlier work. Walter Clemons extolled her "exhilarating literary performance," while also suggesting that Sontag was at the peak of her powers. Geoffrey Wolff called *Illness as Metaphor* "tone-perfect, a gorgeous tough clear piece of writing."[2] For such critics, the quality of the writing itself, its status as literature, was paramount—not the soundness of Sontag's argument in all respects. They took for granted what Sontag said about herself in interviews and to herself in diaries: She was a polemical writer, pushing a set of ideas as far as possible, which would naturally mean that others, and Sontag herself, might well return to her arguments with objections and corrections. *Illness as Metaphor* as a work of literature had an internal consistency and aesthetic, no matter what further developments in science and the arts might do to qualify her conclusions.

When *AIDS and Its Metaphors* appeared more than a decade later, Sontag noted that this new disease had usurped cancer as the most dreaded cause of death. At the time Sontag wrote, effective treatments for AIDS were still in the early stages of development so that the very word had become, as cancer had been, the announcement of a death sentence. Now Sontag felt able to refer to her own breast cancer and to share her personal feelings about being caught up in the metaphors that defined the search for a cure as a war. This change to a self-referential prose had begun with stories like "Project for a Trip to China," one of her best work of prose fiction. In her diaries, she sensed a new power in her style when she more directly accessed her own experiences.

Sontag believed the metaphor of war victimized those with cancer, turning them into victims. AIDS patients, like those with cancer in early periods, suffered ostracism and condemnation. As a sexually transmitted disease, AIDS became the target of moralizers who viewed this "plague" as divine punishment for deviants—as homosexuals were deemed. And since the disease first afflicted the gay community, AIDS was wrongly supposed to be a gay malady. This illness once again isolated infected individuals, forcing them into a morbid solitude that was reminiscent of medieval reactions to illness. And because the outcome of AIDS was often lesions and other disfiguring outbreaks on the face, it became especially repulsive in ways that were not true for polio, heart disease, and other life-threatening illnesses. Calling AIDS a plague politicized the disease, making it seem a threat to the body politic—unlike cholera or influenza, for example, which were exempt from moral judgments. Thus the "gay plague" not only separated the sufferers from society, but the term also prevented a more reasoned understanding of how AIDS might be treated. Old fears about the plague's way of decimating a society infected public discussions of AIDS.

Sontag suggests that this kind of metaphorical thinking and moralizing also failed to recognize that AIDS probably existed long before it was officially identified and named as a disease. All sorts of atavistic attitudes about sex seeped into public consciousness, suddenly making the sexual act a potentially life-threatening risk. The 1960s rhetoric of self-fulfillment now seemed foolhardy to some commentators. Countering these efforts to see AIDS in moral or religious terms, Sontag argues that the language making the disease an invader and subverter of traditional values has to be countered with a rhetoric eschewing the resort to military metaphors. In the end, as with other diseases, AIDS will be treatable and perhaps even curable, Sontag concludes.

Unlike *Illness as Metaphor*, *AIDS and Its Metaphors* received an uncertain and even uneasy reception. In part, the reservations about her book were the result of the familiarity of her argument about metaphors. Too little of the actual work to prevent AIDS was acknowledged in her book, Christopher Lehmann-Haupt noted. Charles Perrow came to a similar conclusion. Randy Shilts, an authority on AIDS, believed she had missed an important opportunity to deal with the failures of liberal society to confront the disease. Jan Zita Grover faulted Sontag, as did other reviewers, for not dealing with the significant literature about AIDS, especially works by gay authors.[3]

That Sontag herself was a member of the gay and lesbian community, and that she did not acknowledge as much, angered and devastated many of her readers and close friends of hers, like Richard Howard, who believed her renown and authority might have been put to much greater use if she had used her own understanding of the gay and lesbian world to counter the notions of a gay plague—that AIDS was somehow the result of a promiscuous society that had tolerated same-sex relations to the detriment of the body politic's health. This aspect of the response to the book might be termed underground, since it never appeared in the mainstream publications. In retrospect, frustrations with *AIDS and Its Metaphors* derived in part because Sontag would not deal directly with the world in which her friends were dying. "Sontag's own experience as a bisexual," one biographer notes, "made her text on AIDS look strangely limp and coy. This was perhaps why the book drew such fire from its critics, especially from the gay community."[4]

That Sontag herself felt some pressure to bear witness by invoking her own personal experience is evident in her AIDS story "The Way We Live Now," published four years after *AIDS and Its Metaphors*. This story, taking its title from Anthony Trollope's novel about the Victorian state of mind, is one of Sontag's most brilliant prose productions. It centers on the responses of twenty-six different individuals to a friend who has contracted AIDS. In effect, a whole society is depicted in these varying voices, which dramatize the profoundly different responses to the disease. Because this is a story composed of dialogue, the effect is of an overwhelming immediacy and urgency, even though the afflicted person is never given a name. Instead, he stands for an everyman, a cynosure of illness. The story begins with the first signs of the disease and the efforts to rationalize it, with his friends giving alternative explanations of his illness. The story canvases a community of feeling through the initial prognosis, his treatment, his doctors, the protocols of hospitalization, the endless speculations about his condition, the varying responses to the prospect of death, his moods, and then his steady deterioration—his bleeding gums and pallor—and the feeble hope that he will survive. The powerful, plaintive, and ambivalent voices in this piece have made it easily adaptable to stage presentations. It seems so universal and representative of the contemporary mood that Gardner McFall called the story "an allegory of our time." Howard Hodgkin's accompanying illustrations in the book version of the story enhanced the "thickening atmosphere," Barbara MacAdam observed. The compact and condensed nature of the dialogue also "compressed all that [Sontag] explored in *Illness as Metaphor* and *AIDS and Its Metaphors*," concluded Rosemary Dinnage.[5]

In "The Way We Live Now" Sontag was also attuning herself, once again, to the voices of fiction, fitfully present in her short story collection, *I, etcetera*, and then elaborated in her last two novels. In fiction, she accomplished what she had not been able to do in her nonfiction prose: to thrust herself, her own sensibility, not only into her prose but also into the figure of a narrator that stood for Sontag, creating and reacting to her characters. At its best, this fiction would yield a stronger, more vibrant, and more personal voice, and at its worst, it would succumb, as it did in her last novel, to a self-regarding sensibility unable to embody an entire fictional world.

CHAPTER 5

The Voices of Fiction

Stories and Later Novels

In her diary entry for November 21, 1978, Sontag wrote, "In fiction I can do what I've done in essays, but not vice versa" (470). She did not explain to herself what she meant, but certainly one aspect of her fiction is its essayistic quality even as it is far more personal—more directly autobiographical than any of her essays. Fiction gave her permission to include herself, as she does in *I, etcetera,* her collection of stories. There one learns about her childhood, her marriage, especially the years just after her son, David, was born, her travels, and many of the private feelings that appeared in her diaries. Her fiction approaches the form of a memoir; her essays seem almost studiedly impersonal.

As with many writers, fiction gave Sontag more latitude to say her work was based on her experience and yet was not, exactly, *her* experience, because she had put her autobiography in the service of her stories. She had used herself as material in her fiction, but in her nonfiction she seemed wary of arguing merely from personal experience, as though ideas attached to a personality were less valuable as ideas per se. The one exception, of course, was her political journalism, where she was virtually obliged to deliver opinions that were hers, opinions derived from her travels and participation in public events and discourse. But those political essays did not loosen her style in the way that fiction, especially stories, could. In *I, etcetera* she explores what she called in a diary entry (February 25, 1979) "my 'Cubist' method, telling story from different angles" (483).

"Project for a Trip to China" was composed before Sontag actually traveled there. And as she later admitted in her diary, her China was not the country she visited, but rather a projection of her imagination, the construct of a lonely girl who missed her father, who had died in China. The actual journey there produced almost nothing in the way of writing. In the story, China figures as the elsewhere Sontag would have preferred to be instead of living with M (obviously based on her mother). The story is really about mind traveling, about how the mind composes a world—in this case, out of remnants of her father's existence: a photograph and the few other objects he left behind. The fiction he represents to her is more real than the daily life she has to endure with her dour mother. The primacy of the imagination, the victory of mind over matter, is a familiar theme in Sontag's first two novels, although her narrators in those narratives are so estranged from their environments that their recourse to their own dreams and illusions proves ultimately self-destructive. Why does this not occur in "Project for a Trip to China"? Precisely because Sontag anchors the narrative in herself, an observant child/adult notating not merely her fancies but also the dreary facts of her childhood. She does not turn away from reality so much as she asserts the superiority of her imagination to transcend that reality without ever denying reality the way Hippolyte and Diddy do. What is more, as her own narrator, Sontag is able to probe the nature of literature, of why it is more satisfying than the actual, real materials out of which it is built. Literature itself, the imagination, becomes a subject in this story as it might in one of Sontag's essays, but she does not have to pretend that the literature-reality nexus is just a topic for the intellect. On the contrary, this story is Sontag's story in every sense of the word. It is hard to see how Sontag could have written such fiction at the beginning of her career, since "Project for a Trip to China" depends on the public persona she had already established for herself. Part of the keen interest in this story—which several reviewers regarded as her best—is that she actually trades on her own fame. The story shows why she had to build up her own sense of the world and her place in it. To do otherwise would have meant capitulating to the morose M, who seems in this story to have given up on life, on the expectation of a better world that her daughter so desperately craves to discover by creating it in her own story. This is why the actual China could never measure up to the child's conception of it.

"Debriefing," the second story, centers on Julia, a life-denying character—anorexic and agoraphobic—a stay-at-home like M. Julia seems immobilized by the existential questions she asks. She is bothered by the way people simply conform to the ordinary conceptions of how to live. The suicidal Julia sees such behavior as useless, and the narrator—another Sontag stand-in—is both disturbed by Julia's penetrating intellect and determined to assert the very connections to others that Julia scorns. The tension in the story, however, resides in the narrator's affinity with Julia. Julia speaks for the narrator's darker self. Julia is one of the many doubles that appear in *I, etcetera*. Indeed, Julia is the etcetera, one of the proliferating versions of the self that the Sontag narrators encounter. Julia appeals to the narrator's own sense of disaffection with others, with commonplace ideas. And yet without establishing a connection to others, to the world, the inevitable result is self-annihilation. Sontag's diaries clearly show that she never contemplated suicide herself and that, indeed, the very idea appalled her; and yet she could not let it alone, because she understood that the act of suicide represented a rejection of the world that she understood and even identified with—as she demonstrates in her essay on Simone Weil, a brilliant thinker and a suicide. The idea of a debriefing, of an explanation of a mission accomplished, is given an ironic turn in this story, since Julia's mission is, in effect, to kill herself. The harrowing aspect of this story is that Sontag explores the insane and yet logical behavior of a character like Julia, whose thinking leads her to take her own life.

"American Spirits" puts the questions about human identity, about how a self can both create and destroy a life, into a historical context. Sontag's essay in *Styles of Radical Will* about pornography as a kind of literature that can both free and degrade the self is given a fresh and comic expression in the story of Miss Flatface, who is inspired by Tom Paine to revolt, leave her husband, and go off with Mr. Obscenity in order to reinvent herself along the lines of Benjamin Franklin, who ran away from home in quest of a new self. Miss Flatface's antiseptic husband is contrasted with Mr. Obscenity and his swarthy friends. They represent all that is counter to mainstream, patriotic culture. They like to talk about Communism, miscegenation, and their belief in free love. A man of principle, Mr. Obscenity offers Miss Flatface to his "black chum," Honest Abe, to whom Miss Flatface reports in patriotic fashion. The range of reference in this story—from Henry Adams, Stephen Crane, and James Fenimore Cooper to William James and Fatty Arbuckle, as well as Edith Wharton and Ethel Rosenberg—suggests the pervasiveness of Sontag's effort to show how perverse the American urge for the pursuit of happiness can become. Indeed, this pursuit becomes a veritable orgy that only serves to make Miss Flatface feel "terribly alone" (e-book location 705), especially since she realizes she has become no more than a sexual object for the gratification of her male masters. This feminist aspect of Sontag's fiction is a new development that heralds her focus on women in her last two novels, a reversal of her penchant for subsuming herself in male voices in *The Benefactor* and *Death Kit*. Indeed, Miss Flatface seems determined to bank on the male gaze by turning herself into a prostitute, although the spirits of William Jennings Bryan and Leland Stanford deplore her low prices for services rendered. But at least she eludes various characters that would seduce and enslave her. She declares herself a "free woman," which not only liberates her from prostitution but also fosters her falling in love for the first time. But this fantasy of married life with Arthur turns poisonous when she eats a bad taco—a comment on the country's fast food fetish, a signal that instant gratification does not equal a seriously satisfying pursuit of pleasure. Laid out in the Easy Come Easy Go Funeral Home, a pun on both the life and the sexual encounters that have dominated Miss Flatface's life, she is last seen in heaven watching with approval as her two ex-husbands grieve over her death. The contrast with Julia's fate, with her denial of sexual connection—indeed her denial of fleshly appetite—is ironic, especially since these two characters, from opposite directions, succeed, haphazardly, in extinguishing their own lives.

"The Dummy" arises in part out of Sontag's interest in science fiction and her groundbreaking essay "The Imagination of Disaster," which is included in *Against Interpretation*. As the title of her essay suggests, science fiction, in its broadest sense, is about the dread of apocalypse, of an end to the world that may be avoidable, or may not. How to cope with that knowledge becomes in "The Dummy" a narrator's effort to create a double of himself, one that will allow him to observe, and thus preserve, himself. After observing his "dummy" on the job, the narrator exclaims, "What a hard life I led!" (e-book location 1046) The trouble is that the dummy falls in love with a secretary, Miss Love, and threatens suicide when his creator says he cannot leave his wife for the other woman. The only solution seems the creation of a dummy for the dummy. And this outcome works surprisingly well, with the narrator and his "relatives" solving the "problems of this one short life" (e-book location 1046). Of course, that is the point: The self cannot really split itself off into other selves, except in the world of fiction, where the very idea of a self, and the pressures to be a self, engenders the creation of other selves. It is as if Sontag is saying that the only solution to selfhood is fantasy or science fiction. This short story is essentially a comic inversion of the suicide narrative of her first two novels.

"Old Complaints Revisited" is a rather murky monologue featuring a translator who wants to leave "the organization" but cannot. He is like a Kafka character who cannot quite fathom the source of his anxiety. He enjoys the sense of exclusivity that comes with membership in a group, even though the group is a party of error. Although the organization is never named, the story reads like a Cold War narrative, the account of a Communist Party member who remains in the fold even after realizing the folly of his membership. The party has become the basis of the individual's identity, and to forsake the party, or in this case the organization, is to abnegate that identity. And then there are the distinguished writers who still belong to the organization, and there is its history to consider, as well as its virtues and vices. In effect, the story is about the sense of belonging and the need for it. Group membership can be comforting insofar as one does not have to act by oneself, and yet the urge to declare independence is also undeniable even as the very idea of exile is forbidding. Part of the problem is translation. How to put into words what the narrator feels? Whatever the narrator declares can only be partially true insofar as words cannot represent the whole person. In the end, it is life itself, the organization of life, that seems to trouble the narrator, who cannot translate its meaning. One way to read this story is as a gloss on Sontag's famous essay "The Aesthetics of Silence," which probes the inadequacy of language and the inability of the artist to say, in words, precisely what he means, or to convey a sense of life with which words can never be commensurate. *I, etcetera,* as its title announces, is a book of self-reflexive fiction, fiction that is about itself, and the fraught ways in which language both creates and destroys or distorts the world—language as merely a translation of the original: life itself.

The clashing and coordinating voices of "Baby," the parents of the child in question, seems a warm-up for the orchestration of varied voices in "The Way We Live Now." A child's anxious parents visit a psychiatrist on alternating days to talk about their boy, although the details they reveal about his life match those of Sontag's own upbringing. Baby's voice is never heard directly and, in fact, he seems unreal insofar as he is projection of his parents' conflicting testimony. Both parents become obsessed with a child who has a mind of his own, a mind that feels threatened by his parents, a "baby" who plots to poison them. The trouble seems to be that he is their "baby"—that is, a projection of their paranoid fears. So perverse is their obsession with their own child, with their idea that they are under threat, that they decide to dismember him. In this cruel parable of childrearing and popular notions of talk therapy, Sontag skewers the psychologizing of family life that results in yet another form of mutually assured self-destruction.

In yet another angle on the idea of the double, "Doctor Jekyll," a surrealistic version of Robert Louis Stevenson's *Dr. Jekyll and Mr. Hyde,* one of Sontag's favorite childhood stories, concentrates on Dr. Utterson, the director of the "Institute for Deprogramming Potential Human Beings." Like "Debriefing," deprogramming deals with the unraveling of the self, of its splitting apart into the eventual disaster that science fiction imagines. Utterson seems to be the author of the story, of the events that follow, insofar as he merges with Dr. Jekyll, although everything in the story is conjectural: "It is possible that a line extends from the flattish back of Utterson's head to Jekyll's striped tie" (e-book location 2289), suggesting that Jekyll is Utterson's projection. As Poague and Parsons suggest in their annotated bibliography of Sontag's work: "The complexity of the twenty-four unnumbered segments of 'Doctor Jekyll' resists sequential annotation. A given segment might link two spatially distant characters—usually Utterson and Jekyll—in a kind of 'subjunctive' doubling."[1]

In effect, the story denies the possibility of biography, of chronology, as a way of explaining human character. To rewrite Stevenson is to acknowledge the modern atomizing of the self, with Jekyll at one point suggesting that he can only complete himself by going off with Hyde, who accuses Jekyll of a homosexuality Hyde rejects. And since Jekyll and Hyde are facets of the same personality as now reimagined by Utterson, there seems to be no way out of the labyrinth of a self that denies part of its own identity.

As the concluding story, the aptly named "Unguided Tour," implies, the self is decentered, fractured into a number of different voices that all go traveling, so to speak, as Sontag does in her opening story. The changing scenery does nothing to allay the uneasy recognition that nothing has changed, as narrators—male and female—swap observations that are difficult to attribute to one voice since no quotation marks are used. As Poague and Parsons observe, the difficulty of distinguishing among speakers suggests that the dialogue is really an internal monologue—a final discourse on "I, etcetera," in which the self cannot contain itself but must double and split off and argue with itself, as Sontag so often said that she did in her essays. The tour can have no guide any more than the self can have a program or a briefing that will clarify the quest to become a self. The Susan Sontag whose work is a product of so many of her travels to Europe and Asia acknowledges that there can be no guidebook to the world or to the self. And yet, unlike her suicidal figures, the final voice of *Unguided Tour* is not defeated and seems buoyed by the journey itself, declaring that this is not "the end."

What more fitting way to conclude *I, etcetera*'s stories about the indeterminacy of the world, which can be harrowing but also exhilarating, than by announcing that like the tour, the book itself can, properly speaking, have no end, no false conclusion that can reassuringly resolve this volume's upsetting but also stirring antinomies?

Reviewers like Anatole Broyard praised Sontag's probing of the problematic nature of language and the writer's efforts to capture reality. Others like Daphne Merkin admired Sontag's daring experimental fictions but deemed some of them failures. Todd Gitlin, in the *Progressive,* faulted the collection for its incoherence and lack of historical context. Novelist Anne Tyler put the case somewhat differently, suggesting that the stories were bold but incomplete, the result of an author too absorbed in herself to provide a satisfying experience for the reader.[2] The fragmentary quality of the stories, in fact, resembles, in certain respects, Sontag's diaries, which would be published posthumously.

Although Sontag would continue to publish short stories, she would not again attempt a major collection of her fiction, turning instead backward toward a kind of woman-of-letters approach in *Under the Sign of Saturn,* a series of portraits of writers who expressed various aspects of herself and who served as models for her own aspirations. Less blatantly autobiographical than *I, etcetera, Under the Sign of Saturn* seems like a mid-career retreat or regrouping of her interest in artist-intellectuals. From here on she experiments only fitfully with the forms of fiction until she discovers the resources of the historical novel, adapting narratives of the past to her modernist sensibility with mixed results.

Although the different voices of Sontag's short stories are admirable efforts to try on all manner of temperaments, in truth, "Project for a Trip to China" proves to be her most enduring accomplishment in *I, etcetera* precisely because she hews so closely to her own voice, playing with her own experience and investing her narrator with a grounding in history that most of her unmoored narrators in both her stories and first two novels lack. Only when Sontag sets her own sensibility against the sweep of history in *The Volcano Lover* and *In America* is she able to give herself permission, after the hiatus following her first two novels, to produce novel-length work. If her desire to subsume the data of the past in her own perceptivity becomes bogged down in the documentary longueurs of *In America,* her ploy seems right to begin with, because, as in her essays, she realizes that her real subject is herself writing and what it means to write. In *The Volcano Lover,* the characters are powerful enough to withstand her prodding and interference; in *In America,* they eventually wear poorly because she is all too attentive to them, so that they become too precious, too much an extension of their author's self-regard. She never quite lets go of them so that they can be themselves.

The Volcano Lover opens with a prologue that introduces the novel's narrator, clearly a contemporary figure with many of Sontag's own interests and tastes. She is dressed casually in jeans and a silk blouse as she wanders through a flea market speculating on where her desire will lead her. The brilliant opening aligns the narrator with her characters—all of whom will be driven by different states of passion. From this perch in the present, the narrator segues to London in the autumn of 1772 and to a meditation on the male and female terms used for volcanoes, and on those who are attracted to danger and those who flee from it. Thus Sontag sets the historical stage for the story of William Hamilton (referred to only as the Cavaliere), his wife, Catherine, his second wife, Emma, and her eventual lover, Lord Nelson (referred to only as "the hero").

Part one centers on the marriage of the Cavaliere and Catherine. In London during his first trip home in seven years, the Cavaliere is making preparations for a return to Naples, where he serves as His Majesty's diplomatic representative. The Cavaliere is a collector, an eighteenth-century man of reason who is nonetheless attracted to the "kingdom of the cinders" (9). Although the narrator does not say so, the Cavaliere is neoclassical man on the verge of transforming himself into a Romantic, driven by his passions as much as by his rationality. His wife, Catherine, seems like the perfect consort for him since her devotion is absolute and his tender care of her is apparent. She does not burn with his desire to explore Vesuvius, but then he does not expect such intensity from her. She has her place in his life just as every piece in his collection has.

Contrasted with the Cavaliere is the king of Naples, a glutton and an ignoramus. If the Cavaliere easily abides the king's vulgarity, it is because of the Cavaliere's aloof nature and sense of duty. So long as he is free to collect his Etruscan vases and other precious objects, the Cavaliere seems quite content at the Naples court. He does not share Catherine's revulsion—even when at the opera the king starts throwing food at his subjects. The Cavaliere takes his role as courtier so seriously that he does not balk at following the king to his toilet, where the king empties his bowels. Indeed, the Cavaliere also accompanies the king on his hunts, which really amount to slaughtering parties. Unconcerned about the ignorant court he attends, the Cavaliere is content with the status quo, even though the revolution in France threatens to spread to parts of Italy, including Naples.

And yet the Cavaliere's uneasiness is apparent in his scenes with Efrosina Pumo, a tarot card reader. He scoffs at her prognostications, but he returns repeatedly to read his fate in the cards. These scenes are an indication that he is not quite as certain of himself or what will happen to him as he imagines. Indeed, the volcano is an obvious symbol of volatility. As Efrosina Pumo tells him: "The future is a hole. . . . When you fall in it, you cannot be sure how far you will go" (53). The Cavaliere, as collector, takes possession of his world, but as the narrator notes, collections also "isolate" (27).

The Cavaliere's life is about to change because the asthmatic Catherine weakens, even though he tries to divert himself with a pet monkey. This "littlest citizen" (76), as the Cavaliere calls the creature, stimulates a sadistic streak in his master, who enjoys taunting the monkey even as he becomes attached to the pet. As the Cavaliere becomes absorbed in the monkey's mimicry and volatile emotions, Catherine finds comfort in the visit of the Cavaliere's second cousin, William Beckford, who becomes her "soul mate and shadow son" (85). They are lovers of literature and unite around their reading of Goethe's novel *The Sorrows of Young Werther* (1774), one of the founding texts of the Romantic period, establishing the central role of passion in the hero's life and the brooding nature that results in his suicide. Like the Cavaliere, the seemingly sedate Catherine is in fact a kind of transitional figure, on her way to becoming a Romantic. Only her sense of decorum and her place as the Cavaliere's wife restrain her passion for Beckford. When Beckford departs, his letters seek to console Catherine, but she slowly succumbs to her illness and dies. A surprised Cavaliere then realizes how deeply he loved his wife, and in his sorrow believes he will never be able to love again.

In part two, the Cavaliere accompanies Catherine's body back to England. He carries with him a prized possession that would later become known as the Portland vase because he sells this item to the Duchess of Portland. As much as such objects mean to him, they are also at his disposal when he is in need of money to support his collecting habit. Up to this point the Cavaliere has been in complete control of himself and his interests, bargaining up the price of collection when necessary, and intent on amassing yet other treasures. His nephew Charles, hoping to inherit the Cavaliere's fortune (in truth it is not nearly as much as Charles supposes), turns over to his uncle his mistress, Emma, since Charles is courting a rich heiress. Emma, unaware of Charles's plans, comes to Naples thinking her stay is but a visit. She writes long, plaintive letters to Charles, who does not answer; and she is shocked when the Cavaliere, smitten with her beauty, makes advances. She stubbornly refuses to believe her shrewd mother, who understands that Charles has abandoned her daughter and placed her in proximity to the Cavaliere for the Cavaliere's pleasure. Emma, although taken aback, is grateful for the Cavaliere's attentions, gradually capitulating to his desires and, in taking on the role as his mistress, begins to exhibit diplomatic skills that serve the Cavaliere well, especially with the queen of Naples, who is much smarter than her husband. Life at court becomes ever more pleasurable for the Cavaliere now that the queen treats Emma as a confidant. Emma quickly learns the Neapolitan language and is admired for her great beauty (she has been painted many times by Romney, who regards her as his favorite model). Emma's stock at court rises as she learns to impersonate various important historical figures in scenes called "attitudes." Only Goethe, on a visit to Naples, seems immune not only to Emma's charms but also to a court life he deliberately rejects, as though to emphasize that the romance that others invest in his novel are not those of its author, who remains aloof and unamused. More than once, as in the novel's final monologues, Sontag introduces a character that has the effect of destroying the romantic aura of her characters and the solipsism of their passions.

At the same time, both Vesuvius and Europe seem to be erupting, and life at court becomes more fretful as the course of the French Revolution seems to threaten the very idea of monarchy even as Emma becomes more celebrated for posing as Medea, Niobe, and Joan of Arc, among other mythic and historical women. The Cavaliere, overcome with love for Emma, does the unthinkable: he marries her, a commoner with a dubious past as a kept woman. And yet she thrives at court and makes the Cavaliere's world a "theatre of felicity" (177). She solidifies his relationship with the king by becoming indispensable to the queen. Yet the queen dreads the fate of her sister, Marie Antoinette, in France, and worries about the loyalty of her Neapolitan subjects.

A new character enters, Lord Nelson, as "the hero," victor of the Nile, who set back the French revolutionary advance. Imbued with a sense of his own historical importance, the hero befriends the Cavaliere and his wife. Already they look to him for protection as the Cavaliere begins to make arrangements to save his collection should the revolutionaries capture Naples. And Emma comforts the queen as conflicts between royalists and republicans intensify. The king, ignoring the precarious state of his rule, continues to hunt while the Cavaliere takes inventory of his collection, not knowing what will happen as the Neapolitan army marches on Rome. The hero, honored by the Neapolitan court, is also regarded as its savior.

The Cavaliere's treasures are sunk on the way to England, and from Palermo the English exiles amuse themselves with parties, cards, and gossip. Emma, still fond of the Cavaliere, becomes enthralled by the hero and begins to behave outlandishly—as far as the English exiles are concerned. Even worse, the hero becomes an object of scornful criticism back home among his superiors. The Cavaliere, who no longer has sexual relations with Emma, tolerates her infidelity—in part because he is as devoted to the hero as she is. Even so, the aging Cavaliere is becoming irrelevant and now clearly an adjunct to any event that includes the hero and Emma. The characters in this triangle all seem at one remove from the reality represented by Baron Vitellio Scarpia, an agent of the king, who is as skeptical of the aristocracy, and those members of it who sympathize with the republicans, as he is of the people. Scarpia calmly stands by as a mob flays a duke, dismembering him and then roasting him alive. While the French take Naples, the court, the Cavaliere, and his wife retreat to Palermo. Scarpia bides his time—and indeed the revolutionaries retreat at the onslaughts of Cardinal Ruffo's peasant army.

Now comes the period of reaction when the hero arrives in Naples to punish the revolutionaries, even though Ruffo has made peace terms guaranteeing their safety and removal to exile. Emma becomes the hero's translator and is blamed for his revoking of Ruffo's terms of peace. The narrator depicts the hero as devoid of common decency and in violation of the rules of war as he consigns so many to be hanged. The hero's superiors are aghast at reports of his affair with Emma and his unprofessional and immoral behavior. As the narrator exclaims: "Eternal shame on the hero!" (296). The consequences of his cruelty are given in graphic detail. The hero remains implacable. But the Cavaliere is out of favor and is summarily recalled to England, his replacement as envoy a young man fresh from his first diplomatic posting. Rumors spread that the hero had become besotted with Emma and lingers in Naples while the French solidify their victories. Emma, already quite fat and no longer beautiful, is pregnant and seeks to hide her condition by the clever use of shawls.

The hero, with both Emma and the Cavaliere in tow, brazenly arrives in England to a rousing welcome from the British people but a decidedly cool reception from his superiors. He dines with his wife and Emma, much to the shame of his wife, and then the hero publicly snubs his wife and hardly makes an effort to conceal his infatuation with Emma. And yet he remains—as is shown in his appearance at a Drury Lane theater—the favorite of a grateful and admiring public. During this period an Irishman shatters the Portland vase, which is painstakingly put back together—in a way that lives cannot, the narrator pointedly observes. Somehow Emma is able to keep up public appearances dancing the tarantella in a way that suggests "pure energy, pure defiance, pure foreboding" (349). Part two ends with the Cavaliere growing enfeebled. He retires to a farmstead in Surrey, dying and dreaming about his losses.

Part three initiates the first of several monologues, a device that Sontag will repeat in *In America,* to express the shifting perspectives of biography and history, the role of the individual witness, and the concatenation of events that otherwise subsume and overwhelm individuals. It is as if she seeks to disrupt historical narratives, which tend to flatten out the role of individuals, making them seem only vessels of the moment, and restore to her characters the vitality of their contributions to history. The delirious Cavaliere on his deathbed recalls and sometimes distorts his memories, confusing and conflating people and events, as he remembers his wife, Catherine, the roles of Emma and the hero in his life, the drawing power of the volcano, his mania for collecting, his waning energy, and his personal extinction. He thinks of Pliny the Elder, who perished in Vesuvius, and then muses on his own place in history: "I would like to be remembered for the volcano" (370). This part, as in the previous parts, begins with one of the plates from the *Collection of Etruscan, Greek and Roman Antiquities from the Cabinet of the Hon. Wm. Hamilton,* as if Sontag is honoring Hamilton's dying wish.

Part four concludes the novel with a series of monologues, beginning with Catherine, who can now speak for herself and not just as a projection of the Cavaliere's own account. She demonstrates that she was quite aware of her role as faithful wife, and how she had an almost ascetic sensibility but was aroused by her love of the Cavaliere, although she subdued her passion in response to his self-contained personality. She expresses a discontent, however, that her husband never imagined. She is disturbed by how women are thought to be different from men, and though she is no feminist or rebel, her uneasiness is palpable. "I should be able to imagine a life without him, but I cannot" (378), she admits. This confession from the grave is rather like the monologues in Sontag's play, *Alice in Bed,* in that a conflicted feminine consciousness is probed, and the reasons why women do not go out into the world are canvassed from a point of view that suggests how estranged women have been in a world dominated by men.

The next monologue by Emma's mother, Mrs. Cadogan, reveals the consciousness of a woman far more worldly than Catherine. Mrs. Cadogan is devoted to her daughter but also recognizes that she cannot control Emma's singular appetite for worldly experience or Emma's belief that she can master whatever comes her way. Mrs. Cadogan understands much more quickly than Emma did that Charles Greville never meant to marry Emma and that he has pawned her off on the Cavaliere. And Mrs. Cadogan watches in amazement and admiration as her daughter surmounts her disappointment over Charles and makes a place for herself in the Cavaliere's life and at the Neapolitan court. Mrs. Cadogan seems an especially reliable witness because she is entirely unaffected and quite willing to acknowledge her misperceptions and mistakes—as in her decision to marry a man who abandons her. She keeps his name as a prudent move that maintains her respectability. This woman of the world understands that her daughter simply cannot resist the "little admiral" (394), an amusing phrase that strikingly brings "the hero" down to earth, as he is seen by a woman who does not engage in hero worship even as she recognizes why others do. It is through Mrs. Cadogan that news of the hero's death is first announced, making this historic event more of a domestic disaster for a mother and daughter whose circumstances will now be greatly reduced.

Emma's monologue follows as a kind of brief for her life and the magical aura that seemed to envelop her even as her critics decried her power over men. Emma credits herself with a power to listen and to become absorbed in lives of those she loved, which leads to her plight as scapegoat when the hero dies. She seeks exile in France of all places because England will not have her. Despite having been brought down in shame after her worldly success, Emma seems without self-pity or guilt about her actions and content with the part she had to play in history, although history—its meaning and consequences—hardly enters her consciousness.

The novel ends in a two-part monologue in which the first, the memoir of a poet, describes her fate as a revolutionary hanged in Naples. She goes to her execution without regret and with a sense of dignity that rebukes the dishonorable actions the narrator has deplored. In the second part, Eleonora de Fonsea Pimental, whose republican and revolutionary statements have been contrasted with the hero's reactionary policies, restores to this part a historical consciousness as well as the mentality of a writer who has stood alone, separated from her husband, rejecting her royal patrons, publicly proclaiming an Ode to Liberty. She has spurned the life of privilege and scorned the way others accommodate to those in power, becoming adept at "abjection" (415). She refuses to become cynical about the power to do good even as she articulates her "hatred and contempt" (416) for the hero. Although this is the concluding monologue, Pimentel is by no means the authoritative voice. For example, she dismisses the Cavaliere as an "upper-class dilettante" (416) and Emma as a "nullity" (417)—judgments that are surely not the narrator's, or the novel's last word on these figures. Instead, Pimental's monologue serves as a demonstration of feminist rage by a writer who specifically condemns the neglect of women's education and their rights. Nevertheless, her last words do cast a forbidding light on the novel's main characters: "They thought they were civilized. They were despicable. Damn them all" (417).

It is not surprising that such an ambitious and daring novel provoked many different kinds of reactions. Daniel Max suggested that Sontag used the historical setting as a way of dealing with "contemporary social and political concerns." He was not impressed, concluding that the novel is "carried off with little heart." On the other hand, novelist A. S. Byatt praised the narrator's "detached, energetic curiosity." For all the absurdity of certain historical events, the novel achieved a "tragic dignity." In sum, Byatt lauded a "slippery, intelligent, provocative and gripping book." Michiko Kakutani admired the work's "intimate and friendly voice" and its "firm moral and political point of view." Maria Warner seemed especially impressed with the concluding female dialogues, although only the Cavaliere seemed to "win the author's own allegiance," Warner concluded. Similarly John Banville, a well-regarded historical novelist, deemed the Cavaliere Sontag's finest achievement, although he slighted the novel as "old fashioned" and thought it was "curiously hollow." Another novelist, David Slavitt, announced his verdict in the title of his review, "Susan Sontag Creates a Bold Historical Romance that Finally Mocks Itself." Richard Eder said that *The Volcano Lover* was "both great fun and serious fun." He noted the irony of the superior Cavaliere, the collector becoming one of the collected.[3]

As to the form of the novel, Rhoda Koenig suggested that Sontag's philosophical asides interrupted and jarred the narrative—as did Jonathan Keates and Evelyn Toynton, who deplored the novelist's "suffocatingly humorless" prose and her "string of verdicts and summations." R. Z. Sheppard disliked the final female monologues, claiming that "Sontag, like Vesuvius, simply blew her top." L. S. Klepp thought Sontag's hatred of the hero destroyed the romance plot and unbalanced the novel. David Gates, on the other hand, extolled the novel's "small, smart details" and the last monologues but deplored Sontag's "amateurish" narrative. John Simon suggested that Sontag had written an "anti-romance," which misfired because of so many contradictory aphorisms. In answer to Banville, Francis L. Bardacke, saw Sontag's "deromanticizing" as the best way to subordinate the hero so that the love triangle with the Cavaliere and Emma remained credible. Putting *The Volcano Lover* in the context of her career as a fiction writer, Bernard F. Rodgers noted how Sontag's expansive polyphonic narrative differed from the interiority of her first two novels.[4]

In a note on the copyright page of *In America,* Sontag notes that the inspiration of her novel is the life and career of Helena Modrzejewska, a nineteenth-century Polish actress who emigrated to America in 1876 and settled there with her husband, Count Karol Chapowski, and their fifteen-year-old son, Rudolf. She was surrounded by a colony of friends, including the future Polish Nobel laureate Henryk Sienkiewicz. Sontag does not disclose the sources she drew on—a decision that later spelled trouble when she was accused of plagiarism. Indeed, she arrogates to herself an absolute freedom from sources, insisting that much of what she has written is her own invention.[5]

Perhaps this insistence on originality for material that has its provenance in history is why Sontag begins *In America,* as she begins *The Volcano Lover,* with a preface in which the narrator takes possession of the story. In this case, however, the narrator is even more strongly identified with Sontag herself, since the narrator, like her creator, grows up in Arizona and California, with Marie Curie as the ideal figure the narrator wishes to emulate, much as Sontag did in her earliest ambition to be a scientist and humanitarian. Sontag even incorporates a recognition that she first made in her diary, dramatizing that entry by writing in the novel that at eighteen she read *Middlemarch* and "burst into tears because I realized not only that I was Dorothea, but that, a few months earlier, I had married Mr. Casaubon" (24)—that is, Philip Rieff. Sontag's narrator has been to Sarajevo (the novel is dedicated to "my friends in Sarajevo") and mistakes at first the Poles she hears in a room of her imagination as Bosnians, since both peoples have suffered occupation and partition.

This preface, titled "Zero," perhaps because it lies outside the novel's narrative, is meant, it seems, to suggest an affinity between the author and her material, or even that the characters (their historical actuality notwithstanding) are truly figments of her imagination not to be confused with their real-life originals. In effect, Sontag is trying to subvert the traditional argument against historical fiction: that the genre is not viable as an independent and autonomous art because its characters derive from a realm outside of the fiction itself. Sontag is arguing, in effect, that the characters are not true to history but only to her own sensibility and historical consciousness. It is a slippery maneuver, however, since that consciousness, as with the figures in *The Volcano Lover,* does have a stubborn extrafictional existence no matter how much Sontag believes she has co-opted them into her narrative. What is more, she will, like most historical novelists, cram in all sorts of detail derived from sources outside the novel. She cannot shuck from her novel the bits and pieces of characters who are, in part, composites of the history she has absorbed. To put it another way, Sontag's historical consciousness cannot be considered entirely apart from the historical data she has sifted and amalgamated for her own purposes. Other novelists, such as Joyce Carol Oates in *Blonde,* have acknowledged their indebtedness to history by including an extensive list of sources, which is to acknowledge as well that her story is not entirely separate from those sources but arises out of the very stuff of history the novelist has attempted to reimagine and reinterpret.

"Zero" suggests that Sontag is returning to her beginnings in California even as her novel tells the story of a woman who wishes to make a new beginning for herself in the West. Sontag's Maryna, like Sontag herself, is not content with her early success or with her status in a troubled land and moves across continents in search of her own salvation. She has Sontag's charisma, the power of attraction that is apparent in the many letters that her admirers and lovers, female and male, sent to her, and that inspired the artist Joseph Cornell to make one of his famous boxes in tribute to her, a diva who commanded the world stage from California to Europe much as Sontag's Maryna does in *In America.*[6] But curiously, the narrator of "Zero" appears only once and then only briefly in the narrative proper. As a result, the interaction between the narrator, characters, and history that is such an integral part of *The Volcano Lover* is absent—and to the detriment of *In America.*

Chapter one begins with some of Maryna's friends doubting the wisdom of leaving Poland for a new life in a farming commune in America. Can she really give up the stage and the recognition it brings, not to mention her devotion to Poland, now under occupation by the Russians, the Prussians, and the Habsburg Empire? At the same time, she is seconded by a devoted following of friends, including Ryszard, who hopes that by accompanying her to America he will win her love despite the presence of her doting husband, Bogdan. Maryna wants to jettison fame and create a new self.

Chapter two explores Maryna's reasons for leaving, her desire to liberate herself in a free country, to make a future for her son Piotr that is not possible in Poland, and her insatiable quest for adventure. That both Bogdan and Ryszard are quite willing to accompany her only solidifies her desire to forge a new identity, one that is not dependent on her Polish audience or the demands of her patriotic contemporaries. She can do no more for Poland, she implies, but there is still much she can do for herself. She is, in fact, tired of dealing with the expectations of others and is willing to risk everything for a fresh start.

In chapter three, Ryszard and his friend, the critic Julien, also a friend of Maryna's, form an advance party, traveling to America in preparation for her entrance. Here Sontag explores the world of steerage that Ryszard wishes to write about on his way over to America. Below decks the boat teems with poor immigrants, including a woman who sells her body to the Polish writer, who is ashamed of their assignation but also fascinated with her plight, as Maryna would be, he assures himself. The episode aboard ship seems a set piece to contrast the cramped and desperate nature of the journey to America with the arrival in New York City, which seems to contain elements of "everywhere." It is there that Ryszard sees a poster touting California as the laborer's paradise.

Maryna arrives in Manhattan in chapter four, making friends in the Polish community and dining at the famous Delmonico's. She accompanies her son Piotr to the Centennial Exhibition in Philadelphia. Everything is still a wonder to her, and she admires the unfinished quality of the country. Everything is still "under way" (147). To abandon acting, she asserts, is to leave behind the make-believe of bravery. Now she has an opportunity to act on quite another stage. But in chapter five, that new platform, Anaheim, California, represents not so much the reality of America as a utopia, the location of her dreams of unified, collective action of the kind not possible in Poland. She wants her commune to be self-supporting. She claims not to miss the theater and to be entirely com-mitted to living off the land and "being stripped" (173) of her former self so that she can rebuild her life on new principles.

But the actual administration of the farm is a daunting task for Maryna's Polish converts, who find an agricultural economy precarious and the work tiring. Maryna has trouble adjusting, especially when her son insists on a new name: Peter instead of Piotr. Maryna resists because the new name is Russian to her, but eventually she relents when her son steadfastly remains aloof until she accedes to his wish. Part of the problem is that her followers still regard her as a queen of the stage, and their sojourn in California takes on an unreal quality—a momentary diversion from her life's work as a performer. An excur-sion with Ryszard, who briefly becomes her lover, also signals the end of the commune, when Maryna not only desires to return to the stage but to conquer a new audience in America. As Bogdan points out, what Maryna wanted all along was a renewal of herself; the farm, the commune, America, were all a pretext. But in returning to Bogdan, she also forsakes Ryszard, realizing that she needs her husband by her side as she relaunches her career.

In San Francisco, in chapter seven, Maryna engages Miss Collingridge to im-prove the actress's English pronunciation, and she auditions for Angus Barton, a theater impresario. At this point, Sontag begins to tread on the ground Mark Twain brilliantly explored in his depiction of American eccentrics. If Maryna is to become an American star, she must jettison certain mannerisms, Barton advises, because audiences "don't want a steady diet of lady" (241). But she triumphs over his skepticism and realizes that she can live fully only on the stage. Or, as she tells Ryszard, who continues to pursue her without more success: "I never know exactly what I feel when I'm not on a stage" (290). She lives to act.

In chapter eight, Maryna returns for a visit to Poland, but her place now is in America, where she embarks on a grueling cross-country tour. She also tries a series of performances in London and is well received, but without the kind of accolades she had become used to as an American star and as the great Sarah Bernhardt's rival. Maryna is in such demand and her tours are so profitable that her manager has her own railroad car fitted out so that she can travel in style and comfort. But what to do with Maryna at this point seems uncertain—at least this is one interpretation of how Sontag decides to end the novel. Chapter nine concludes Maryna's story with a long monologue by Edwin Booth, American's greatest actor, who is haunted by the infamy of his brother John Wilkes Booth, Abraham Lincoln's assassin. The jaded Booth hectors Maryna in a very unpleasant, nonstop speech, telling her how to act, saying that she lacks a sense of tragedy (a bizarre comment to an actress from partitioned Poland), and, in sum, dictating how she should treat him. Except for a few instances where Maryna's gestures or a few words of hers serve to placate Booth, why this monologue should become the novel's ending is not clear. Perhaps like the monologues in *The Volcano Lover*, Sontag is content with an ironic commentary on what has gone before in the narrative, but in this case Booth's insulting sarcasm is very hard to take as other than a mockery of Maryna's own quest to establish a new identity. Booth, in other words, takes his place in a gallery of tiresome American characters who seem to reflect the disdain for America that Sontag evinces in so many of her articles and interviews.

In America received a much more problematic reception than did *The Volcano Lover*, although it won the National Book Award. Sarah Kerr had a high opinion of the novel, although the ideas seemed somehow predigested and lagged behind the characters and scenes. Michiko Kakutani, who had hailed *The Volcano Lover*, expressed her disappointment in a "banal, flat-footed narrative that chronicles the characters' exploits through letters, journals and corny, omniscient voice-overs. 'He was in a dark place,' Sontag writes of one character, 'where there were only wounds.'" John Sutherland was more blunt: "Let's face it: if this was a first novel by a literary unknown it would have been lucky to make it into print." James Woods, considered one of the best literary critics of the last two decades, lauded the novel for its meshing of narrative and history. To Elaine Showalter *In America* was "inert." Michael Silverblatt gave the best rationale for "Zero" and Edwin Booth's monologue, arguing that both were an antidote to Maryna's "lacquered self-deception." If true, though, why was Maryna, who dominates the novel, worthy of so much prose in the first place?[7]

Surprisingly, none of the reviewers noted that Maryna's gift as an actress had to be taken on faith. What, after all, do we learn about her as an actress other than Booth's criticism of her stage work? We learn about the plays in which she performed, but how they were performed and what they say about Maryna remains a mystery. She never really comes alive, *on stage,* which is, after all, where she truly finds herself—as Maryna is the first to confess. Instead Maryna simply stands for the idea of the diva and is something of an abstraction even though she arises out of an actual actress. Somehow, as Adam Begley concluded in the *New York Observer,* Sontag never allows the story to "do its work."[8]

CHAPTER 6

Experiments in Theater

Susan Sontag's work in the theater began as an undergraduate at the University of Chicago, where she met Mike Nichols, who would become a renowned theater and film director, and where she worked on theater productions. She includes her *Partisan Review* theater pieces in *Against Interpretation* as well as discussions of avant-garde directors and playwrights. She soon abandoned work as a theater reviewer because so much of what was presented on the American stage displeased her. The tradition of the well-made play and of dramatic realism, in which characters were presented in scenes that were meant to faithfully represent life outside the theater, seemed jejune to her. Even plays that probed human psychology seemed, to her, to avoid the implications of drama that theoreticians and practitioners such as Brecht and Artaud explored.

In 1979, when Sontag directed a play for the first time, she chose Luigi Pirandello's *As You Desire Me*, which purposely played with the very notion that biography or history could define the nature of the main character, Cia. Similarly, Sontag's direction of Milan Kundera's adaptation of a Diderot play, *Jacques and His Master*, dislocated a linear plot. The two principal characters are on a journey trisected by the love stories of Jacques, of his master, and of Madame de La Pommeraye. Each story is a variation on the others. The stories interrupt each other, repeat each other, and complete each other, anticipating Sontag's direction of three sets of Vladimirs and Estragons in her 1993 production of *Waiting for Godot*.

Realism in such stagings was displaced by stylized, intellectualized theater, aimed at undermining bourgeois society's confidence in itself and its ability to interpret human character. Sontag could not abide the philistine confidence of Westerners, especially Americans, whose complacent beliefs form a seemingly impregnable fortress of self-justification. Hence a Susan Sontag production would entail considerable confusion about her characters' identities (Who is the master? Who is the slave?), as if their stories do not really belong to them but are part of the playwright-director's conception of a stage platform that interrogates the very meaning of human character. Thus Sontag was drawn to such writers as Brecht and Artaud, who challenged theater conventions in what Brecht called the "alienation effect," which does not allow the audience to identify with a play's characters. On the contrary, the play itself, the effort of art to express itself, becomes the paramount subject matter.

Sontag began writing for the stage in 1991 with *A Parsifal,* although this play, only six pages long, was not originally intended for production but as a commentary on Wagner's *Parsifal.* This brief tour de force turns the Christian hero on his head, so to speak, since he becomes, as Julia A. Walker notes, "anti-hero . . . incapable of being moved to sympathy." Whereas Wagner's opera is a story of redemption, Sontag's absurdist protagonist is so lacking in admirable traits that he affronts the audience's sensibilities. It is not a hero who must act to save the world but the audience, Walker suggests.[1]

Sontag signaled her disenchantment early in a "Going to Theater" article published in the winter 1964 issue of the *Partisan Review,* where she criticized a production of Carson McCullers's *The Ballad of the Sad Cafe,* suggesting that the director had encouraged the audience to behave as voyeurs wishing to "see a deformed person without being seen back." Like Brecht, she wanted to create a theater that put its audience on the spot, so to speak, and make it uncomfortable. In sum, she sought to destroy the viewer's sense of privilege, of just looking on, as though observing a spectacle. She demanded that the audience become part of what is staged.

Instead of questing for the Holy Grail like a Christian hero, Parsifal appears in a press conference clutching a glowing red microphone. He broadcasts, in other words, only his own fame, although what is implicit in his success, Walker argues, is a condemnation of our own complicity in a world that values fame, not spiritual transformation. Parsifal goes to his execution having saved no one—not even himself. And so *A Parsifal* concludes with the protagonist's contradictory last words and actions, which also call attention to the very artifice of the play itself: "This is a play, this is a death, this is slowness. If we slow down enough we will never die. (*Reaches top of scaffold.*) If we move, we move into the future. We will die. (*Remains motionless. Lights up.*) We will not die."[2] Like the characters in *Godot,* he knows what needs to be done, but he cannot exert himself.

Such gnomic, self-reflexive drama defeats the normal expectations of audiences. Thus it is not surprising that reviewers split over how to react to

Sontag's subversive plays. One critic saw *A Parsifal* as a product of Sontag's camp sensibility, treating the serious Wagnerian opera in an almost frivolous fashion, and yet with a serious intent, with Parsifal appearing as "the leader, an all-too-recognizable politician corrupted by experience, wooed by power, and lulled into meaningless sexual activity."[3] Another critic dismissed the play as appealing only to "Susan Sontag completists," noting that "Ms. Sontag's clueless young Parsifal, confessing his general ignorance early on, says: 'I'm not good at talking. Perhaps I am retarded.' Try wedding that to transporting music, Dick!"[4]

The Very Comical Lament of Pyramus and Thisbe (An Interlude), published in the *New Yorker* (March 4, 1991) and reprinted in *Where the Stress Falls,* is, like *A Parsifal,* a satire—this time taking up a story as old as Ovid and one that has been retold many times, including the interlude in Shakespeare's *A Midsummer Night's Dream.* Sontag's brief play begins with the disappearance of the wall that had separated the two lovers. Without the wall they seem unsure of themselves, as if without an obstacle, without a barrier obstructing their love, they do not know how to regard their relationship. The wall seemed to have presented, like the Berlin wall separating East and West Germany, a way of defining limits—a set of conditions that proscribe behavior. The lovers are free now to meet, to indulge in a consumer society. Behind the wall, each lover had a clearly demarcated identity, but now they are merely part of an undifferentiated mass. Enter the Spirit of New York, predicting the coming capitalist economy and its disparate elements, a cultural mismatch of real estate developers and trendy restaurants, independent films, and "your rude mechanicals" (an allusion to the ludicrous performance of Pyramus and Thisbe in *A Midsummer Night's Dream*). The lovers now are fixated on getting rich. They proclaim themselves free, but free for what? The rapid changes in their lives confuse them. What does freedom mean, what does their love mean, in a world where "everything is for sale" (290).

Alice in Bed (1991), a play about Alice James, sister of psychologist William James and novelist Henry James, is more grounded in history and biography than Sontag's earlier work for the stage. Alice is an invalid dying from breast cancer. Although she is in no position to exert authority over anyone, she has a compelling presence even when she is attended by a nurse and carrying on badinage with her brother Henry. Organized in eight separate scenes, Alice is juxtaposed against her importunate nurse, her aloof father, whom she almost brains with a brick but also consults as to whether she should commit suicide. She seeks but also thwarts Henry's attentions, debates the merits of her secluded life with Emily Dickinson and Margaret Fuller, the former another recluse, the latter a worldly woman who perished in the waters off the New

England coast. Alice also engages in a dialogue with a male burglar, a Cockney, who seems flummoxed by her lack of fear and willingness to part with even her most treasured possessions. In short, Alice has a vivid imagination and strength of mind that is equal to all the other characters in the play, and yet she refuses to get up and engage directly with the world. Hers is the triumph of the imagination, but as Sontag points out in a note to the play, the triumph of the imagination is not enough.

Even though the play is anchored in the life of Alice James, Sontag has freely invented the words she gives to her characters. If she is making a point about how women have been secluded and diminished, her Alice is no simple victim since she is counseled to act by no less than Margaret Fuller (author of America's first great feminist text) and Emily Dickinson (arguably the country's greatest poet). In the genteel setting of a tea party, Alice acts out her conflicted idea of her own femininity, which is also indissolubly connected to her close relationship with her brother Harry (Henry James). And to make the drama more phantasmagorical, Wagner's Kundry and Myrtha (from *Giselle*) make their operatic appearances and articulate through their very presence Alice's options: rebellion or passive acquiescence to her lot. This is also, of course, the tea party world of *Alice in Wonderland,* with the wonderland in this case being the inside of Alice James's imagination.

That Alice James is sovereign in this play is indicated by Alice's saying, "Emily was saying she found it intimidating to be alone with me. Don't you hate it, when someone says that to you" (41). The line refers, of course, to Sontag herself, who often expressed her frustration with those who said they were daunted by her presence. Like Sontag, Alice feels "ambushed. Either you take it as a compliment, and then you're straddling your flatterer whether you want to or not. Or you start reassuring, groveling really, to put the other at ease" (41). Unlike Sontag, Alice cannot get up from her bed and travel. She is, like Parsifal, defined by her stasis. Alice finds no way out of her self-imposed isolation, but the play, so Walker argues, urges the audience, as in *A Parsifal,* to take responsibility for acting on its own behalf. No hero, or in this case heroine, can displace or enact the actions of others.[5]

Alice in Bed treats her invalidism not only as a feminist issue but also as one of the central problems of humanity. What are individuals supposed to do when they get out of bed? Take the world by storm, as Margaret Fuller did? Or should they stay at home, creating a world just as adventurous through the medium of language, as Emily Dickinson did? Sontag seems to ponder everything: what it means to be a woman in the distinguished James family, the nature of language ("tenses are strangely potent aren't they" [26]), the patterns of history, class structure (Alice has a talk with a Cockney burglar), and the paradox of Alice herself, who does not get out of bed and yet says, "My mind makes me feel strong" (97). As with *A Parsifal*, the characters' commentary on their own ideas has drawn ambivalent responses from critics who deem the play more essay than drama, sketchy and superficial.[6]

In 1993 Sontag was invited to stage a play in besieged Sarajevo. She chose to direct *Waiting for Godot,* reasoning that what theatergoers wanted most was not light entertainment that relieved them of their suffering but, on the contrary, a serious drama that articulated their frustration and despair, as they hoped and doubted that the international community, especially the United States, would intervene and stop the war. She decided to perform only the first act of the two-act play and later rationalized her decision, saying that the second act was even bleaker than the first and that she wanted to preserve at least some of the expectation that, in fact, the dire situation in Sarajevo was not beyond salvation. And more than ninety minutes, the time it took to perform the first act, would be beyond the audience's endurance in a theater lit only by candlelight, with both the cast and the audience straining to remain alert after entire days taken up just with procuring water and the other necessities of life.

That Sontag took liberties with Samuel Beckett's text seems not to have troubled her—not even when she tripled the couple, Vladimir and Estragon, so that on stage three pairs of characters were seen: two men at the center, two women on the right, and a man and a woman on the left—"three variations on the theme of the couple" (*Where the Stress Falls,* 304). In an essay about her production, Sontag does not say in so many words what that theme is. But it seems to reflect her wish to show women and men confronting the terrible conditions of their existence with varying degrees of optimism and pessimism and forming couples, or alliances, so to speak, to deal with their common fate.

Sontag's sense of inclusiveness may have been just what her audience craved. David Toole called the production a "collective enterprise," so that Vladimir and Estragon no longer seemed so isolated, which is to say that the play no longer seemed quite so bleak. Another critic, Erika Munk, thought Sontag had made the play too relevant to its environment. She thought the moment at the end the play when the candles were extinguished was too calculated. "I was left dry-eyed," she concluded.[7]

Sontag's adaptation of Henrik Ibsen's *Lady from the Sea* (1999) has rarely been produced. Julia Walker calls Sontag's last play a "female captivity narrative," in which Sontag has her heroine return to her husband, Hartwig, even as Ellida casts doubts on what her return means: "So now that I am free to choose I can even choose you." He agrees, but then she adds: "But will I still be free, Hartwig, if I choose you?" Now his answer is ambiguous: "There are no certainties in freedom."[8] These dramas of irresolution seem to be Sontag's commentary not only on the contrivances of conventional drama—even in the work of a great realist such as Ibsen—but also statements about the precarious autonomy of the individual, a drama that she would enact repeatedly in her diaries.

CHAPTER 7

Impresario of Modern Literature

Under the Sign of Saturn is a worthy nonfiction successor to *I, etcetera.* Although Sontag's collection of biographical/critical portraits only fitfully employs autobiographical allusions, her style nevertheless reflects her own sensibility, a desire to incorporate diverse but compatible writers into her own literary persona—and in one instance, to measure her newfound interest in history against the prevarications of filmmaker Leni Rienfestahl.

Sontag's first essay, "On Paul Goodman," was a surprise—to her and to others when it first appeared. She allowed herself, as never before, to directly engage with her personal response to a writer, which is perhaps why she chose the Goodman essay as the lead to *Under the Sign of Saturn.* Her first responses to Goodman had been consigned to her diaries, published after her death. She noted, seven years before the publication of *Saturn,* this statement from Goodman's *Down in the Mouth* notebook for 1955: "To know an 'objective truth'— this is fairly idle and for the most part a phenomenon of withdrawal from contact" (198). The style of Goodman's prose reflected truth as seen through his own sensibility—the opposite of an academic approach—and a model for Sontag, who wanted to impress herself on her subjects. As she wrote even more revealingly in her diary entry for July 31, 1973: "I'm finally handling / touching autobiographical material directly. The Europeanized voice ('translatorese') of the earlier fiction was the just correlative of the fact that I had transposed— displaced what I was writing about. It started with the Paul Goodman essay— feeling grief, and having the courage (and interest) to advertize [*sic*] it" (358).

In her essay, Sontag claims Goodman is the only American writer to have a major impact on her. Yet, she confesses that she did not like the man. Sontag was not the only one to find him standoffish and prickly. His public appearances could be irritating, and he seemed to take pleasure in baiting his audiences.[1] But for Sontag, Goodman's adversarial stance is admirable and worthy of emulation. She also likes his constant experimenting with fiction and nonfiction—a program of creativity that she also follows. Goodman was attacked for his versatility by those who deplored what Sontag terms his "amateurism," but this is precisely what she extols: his overwhelming desire to filter all phenomena through his own perceptions. Goodman's commitment to ideas, to writing, to all forms of literature is passionate, and that degree of intensity is exactly what Sontag wishes to convey in *Under the Sign of Saturn* and which she announces by deciding to begin with her mixed reactions to Goodman, the man and the writer.

An even more difficult case is Antonin Artaud, an extreme version of Goodman, in a way, because Artaud defines writing itself as an affirmation of the author, not the content of what he is writing about. Even more than Goodman, Artaud expresses Sontag's desire to elevate the idea of writing and the role of the writer above all else in literature. She revels in his style and mind and treats his work as so many fragments of his sensibility. Art is its own justification in Artaud's belief in the symmetry of truth and beauty. No wonder, then, that Sontag supports Artaud's rejection of realism, since the doctrine of the mimetic means a slavish fealty to the world outside of art. At such moments, Sontag seems to recalibrate how she is to portray the artist's dream world that pervades her first two novels. What seems different now is the role she accords to drama, which Artaud regarded as a "total art form," and her attraction to an Artaudian theater that is "carnal, corporeal." Theater reflects Artaud's materialist sensibility, which grounds him in actual experiences and in a revolutionary program that satisfies Sontag's quest to reject realism without succumbing to the solipsism of characters like Hippolyte and Diddy. Artaud's art, in other words, is not lifelike; his art aims, on the contrary, to transform life.

Yet Artaud himself is a kind of failure in Sontag's essay, a theoretician who abandons the stage—or rather makes of his own life a performance and an embodiment of his ideas. This quest to live for his art, no matter how the audience responds, has a deep-seated appeal for Sontag even as she concedes and even seems drawn to an artist who was more than a little mad—almost insane—about ideas that he could not put into practice. Their very impracticality is what seems to make them appealing to her—perhaps because of his staunch refusal to live by the conventional and orthodox thinking of mainstream theater. In Artaud's language, she argues, can be found a liberation from confining concepts, even Artaud's own.

In "Fascinating Fascism," Sontag emulates Goodman and Artaud insofar as she takes an adversarial position not only against feminists and others who have transformed Leni Riefenstahl from Nazi propagandist into an icon of

IMPRESARIO OF MODERN LITERATURE

documentary cinema, but also against her own earlier argument that the form and style of Riefenstahl's infamous *Triumph of the Will* can be appreciated alongside an acknowledgment of her film's appalling politics. The question of aesthetics, of what is beautiful, Sontag now argues, cannot be separable from the moral implications of a work of art. And the moral implications of Riefenstahl's work can only be fully revealed by a discussion of her biography and the filmmaker's place in history.

Sontag begins by demonstrating that Riefenstahl consistently misrepresented her career. All along, as actress, director, and photographer, Riefenstahl adopted a fascist outlook that fastens on the human figure as a source of strength and beauty that outweighs all other considerations. Thus in her early mountain films, Riefenstahl as actress first enacts the fascist triumph of the will over nature, over any obstacle to the assertion of the will. Fascism valorizes the submission to all powerful figures even to the extent of worshipping death in the service of those in power. That the Nuba are Africans is of less concern to Sontag than that Riefenstahl selects aspects of the Nuba that confirm her fascist aesthetic. This glamorizing of strength makes the submission to it all that more enticing in the imagery of human perfection. Sontag interprets the craze for Nazi regalia—especially uniforms—as another example of the conformity and uniformity that appeals to the fascist mentality. Individuality is obliterated by obedience to the all-powerful leader, so that sacrifice to the fascist cause is depicted as an ecstatic experience, a kind of salvation, when, in fact, what is worshipped is death itself.

Sontag's next essay, on Walter Benjamin, continues her probing of the nature of human will. She treats the will almost as a double of the self, the self that is determined by its origins—as in astrology—by a sign but also by the will, which can redefine the self. The first part of her profile is reminiscent of *On Photography,* in which she suggests that photographs of Benjamin conceal as much as they reveal. What he is thinking remains elusive to the camera, and yet his temperament, as reflected in his gaze, turns him into a text that can be read, however tentatively. Sontag's distrust of psychology as a key to human character is reflected in her attraction to Benjamin's description of himself in terms of an astrological sign, so that he appears as saturnine. But is his melancholic disposition a given, she wonders, or is it a product of his determination not to be defined by his urban existence? And is this resistance to be understood as also part of a more general refusal of "interpretation wherever it is obvious" (122)? This last phrase shows how Sontag has attached herself to Benjamin, fusing his contrary way of thinking to hers. Like her, Benjamin—or is it like him?—suggests that photographs are appealing because they are enigmatic, miniatures of a larger world that evades analysis. In this realm where Benjamin cannot fix on a single self, writing becomes his primary form of creating himself (as it does for Sontag) and also deconstructing himself, since, again like Sontag, so much of his writing is a quarrel with himself. It is finally Benjamin's openness to alternative arguments that Sontag covets for herself.

From photographs of Benjamin that prove to be indeterminate evidence, Sontag turns to Hans-Jurgen Syberberg's *Hitler, A Film From Germany,* which explores the antinomies of art and human character that bemuse her. Neither a work of realism in the documentary mode, nor of the kind of spectacle that dominates Riefenstahl's *Triumph of the Will,* Syberberg presents Hitler himself as product and shaper of film, including the newsreels he watched during the war, becoming, in a sense, his own moviemaker. Syberberg seems to suggests in his wide-ranging references to Wagner, Brecht, and other artists that Hitler's politics are, in part, an aesthetic phenomenon, a part of German culture out of which he emanated with a kind of debased Romanticism, which led him to think of himself as an individual with a sense of destiny—yet another manifestation of the will that bedevils Sontag throughout *Under the Sign of Saturn.* She suggests that Syberberg has a Wagnerian ambition to dominate the medium of film as the composer dominated opera, and that *Hitler, A Film From Germany* is very much about the hegemony of cinema and Syberberg's effort to encompass both history and the aesthetic representation of it.

Of all the thinkers and writers in *Under the Sign of Saturn,* Roland Barthes seems the most playful and the opposite of the saturnine temperaments that attract Sontag. He holds his own with these other masters because of his simultaneously "combative" and "celebratory" (170) sensibility—a good description of Sontag herself, as she grew more and more comfortable with openly declaring which writers and ideas gave her the most pleasure. Barthes is, for Sontag, the quintessential writer because, *au fond,* that is virtually all he cared about: writing, classifying the world in words, studying, like Sontag, the forms words take, although unlike her, he acknowledged that he had little interest in the moral aspects of art and society, or with politics, except insofar as there is a politics of writing. He cared most about the "dramaturgy of ideas," of how they appear in conjunction with each other. It was, in sum, the play of language that delighted him and that draws Sontag's fond allegiance to his memory. "Remembering Roland Barthes," is an especially apt title since she wishes to capture him in motion, inventing his own language.

In "Mind as Passion," Elias Canetti speaks to another side of Sontag— what she calls the itinerant intellectual, always on the move, seeking ways of dominating the world through words, creating, in his own novel, a main character like Sontag's early suicidal heroes, who carry the world in their heads. Given to aphorism, as is Sontag, Canetti subverted the idea that history is a legitimate form of understanding, perhaps as a result of his own exile in England and his penchant for showing how the mind shapes the world through the energy of language. To the masses, the crowds he wrote so eloquently about, Canetti offered a portrayal of the individual's autonomy and freedom to overturn "reductive habits of thinking" (200). In sum, it is the passion of such a mind that appeals to Sontag and helps anchor the ending of her book.

John Leonard liked Sontag's passion, but he suggested that her insights came larded with too much praise for her subjects. Similarly, Seymour Krim labeled the book "missionary work in behalf of contemporary European culture heroes (and villains)." John Lahr was one of the first of several critics to see *Under the Sign of Saturn* as disguised autobiography, resulting in somewhat distorted views of Walter Benjamin and Artaud but also a shrewd attack on Leni Riefenstahl. Frank Kermode and Jonathan Rosenbaum found Sontag's celebration of writers on the margin as troubling because it said as much and, in some cases, more about Sontag than about her subjects. She had domesticated these artists in agony, David Bromwich argued, and minimized their more destructive attitudes. An uneasy awareness barely broke the surface of reviews that reflected on Sontag's hero worship. How different was Sontag's sensibility from Riefenstahl's Wagnerian Romanticism, a Wagnerian Romanticism that Sontag had honored in Syberberg's Hitler film? In attacking Riefenstahl, Jon Cook pointed out that Sontag was criticizing herself. But was that attack enough, especially in view of Sontag's identification with male intellectuals, a connection that made *Under the Sign of Saturn,* in Cook's estimation, a "*counter*-feminist work." This is precisely what poet Adrienne Rich alleged when Sontag's Riefenstahl essay appeared five years earlier in the *New York Review of Books*. In an exchange with Sontag in a later issue of that same publication, Rich called out "Fascinating Fascism" for failing to link fascism and modernism with patriarchy. Sontag responded with some irritation, reiterating that feminists were in part accountable for reviving Riefenstahl's reputation and for reductive arguments that made fascism and patriarchy synonymous. To do so meant obliterating important distinctions and engaging in an anti-intellectualism that in itself led to fascism.[2]

"Writing Itself: On Roland Barthes," Sontag's introduction to *A Barthes Reader* (a 1982 collection that she edited), reads like an appendix to *Under the Sign of Saturn,* a piece once again designed to promote her dialectical view of the intellectual and intellectual life. In this essay, reprinted in *Where the Stress Falls,* Sontag expands on her view of Barthes as mainly concerned with writing itself, discovering in him an aphoristic style aimed at having the "last word" in a set of maxims that seeks to maneuver around the encrusted body of criticism attached to canonical writers like Michelet and Sade by concentrating on their form and the contours of their work—much as Sontag herself had done in her discussions of writers in *Against Interpretation*. Like the Romanian philosopher E. M. Cioran, Barthes, in Sontag's view, argues against himself—another Sontag ploy—thus keeping all sides of an argument in a fruitful tension. This kind of writing works best in short form, she points out, where arguments are compressed, miniaturized. As in her case, the writer becomes a performer, and what is performed often is a volte-face. Thus the conventional lines of argument are disrupted, occasioning, at least in Barthes's prose, a "festive" (69) atmosphere, whereas writers like Sartre take positions and stake out stances. Barthes, eschewing Benjamin's despairing view of politics, asserts the flamboyant sensibility of the writing self, making his employment of language a heroic activity. Barthes disburdened himself of ideas as much as he acquired them and came to the end of his career (terminated by a car accident) writing a species of autobiography featuring himself as the dismantler of received attitudes and canons of criticism.

Sontag professes to see Barthes's work as complete, even though it concluded abruptly with his death. But she does not ultimately come to terms with his sly and inconclusive prose, or the sense in which his writing may, in some respects, simply be a dodging of responsibility for the positions he wishes to entertain but not, ultimately, to be associated with. Like Sontag herself, Barthes, at least in her accounting of him, seems, finally, thought provoking but also, in certain respects, irresponsible. Of course, Sontag would argue that Barthes's keen attention to ideas, to arguments and counterarguments, is the only way forward for the intellectual.

Sontag notes that in politics Barthes sought to tell truths that other writers ignored—exactly her own tactic in her 1982 Town Hall speech in which she castigated the left for too long ignoring or, worse, rationalizing the perfidies of Communist states. She argued against the leftist notions that it was not the doctrine but the distorted and malign implementation of Marxism that was at fault. And in a true Barthes-like twist, she dispatched Communism as "Fascism with a human face." In contracting her argument into an aphorism, she was emulating the playful language she treasured in his work. And that sense of play arose out of both Barthes's and Sontag's conviction that the modern writer is a performer and what he performs is his writing. Thus she quoted approvingly Nietzsche's prophecy that the modern age will be the age of the actor, the writer who uses a mask as a style of performance that becomes the embodiment of ideas that, as Sontag said in her diaries, are to be discovered through the use of a mask. The consequences of seeing the writer as playing a role are revealed in Sontag's approval of the way Barthes turned on his own work in his last books, taking issue with himself just as Sontag did in

"Fascinating Fascism" when she reversed her verdict on Leni Riefenstahl. Similarly, in a new introduction to *Against Interpretation* (included in *Where the Stress Falls*), she reports that she no longer endorsed her praise of the French new novel and, indeed, never really liked this form of fiction all that much. This kind of volte-face not only did not embarrass Sontag but she positively reveled in it, for she was following Barthes's formula of "all great esthetes . . . of having it both ways" (*Where the Stress Falls*, 81).

What mattered to Sontag, and to Barthes, is where the play of ideas took them, and not whether those ideas could be said to be right then, let alone forever. The aesthete is always moving on, Sontag says of Barthes, which means that ideas are detachable from the writing self who utters them. This self is very French, she emphasizes, because it stands for a "locus of possibilities" (83), not a repository of knowledge. This is the "Jacobin tradition of ruthless assertions and shameless ideological about-faces" (84), as she observes without a seeming qualm.

Where the Stress Falls (2001), Sontag's first major collection of essays since *Under the Sign of Saturn*, does not have that work's coherence. The former is organized as a kind of gallery of intellectual greats and so does not have the dialectical design of *Against Interpretation* and *Styles of Radical Will*. *Where the Stress Falls* is much more of a miscellany, reflecting the occasional nature of pieces written as prefaces and forewords to the work of others and stand-alone articles never meant to occupy any particular place in a unified volume. As a result, the structure of the collection—such as it is—is functional, with headings that are generally and vaguely descriptive: "Reading," "Seeing," "Feelings," "There and Here." Like most compendiums, this one is uneven and repetitive and does nothing to enhance Sontag's reputation as an essayist, even though a few pieces in the volume rank with her best work.[3]

Writing about the Russian poet Marina Tsvetaeva (1892–1941) in "A Poet's Prose," Sontag puts her in the context of poets like her friend Joseph Brodsky, who believed that poetry was the highest form of writing, next to which prose was a "slack mental condition." She refers to him as saying poetry was aviation, prose the infantry. This notion of poetry as the most heroic, the most intense form of expression, the most noble and honest, Sontag asserts, is a product of Romanticism and nineteenth-century Russian literature. As usual, she bends literary history to her sensibility by suggesting that a poet's prose not only has a "particular fervor, density, fiber," but that it also has a "distinctive subject: the growth of the poet's vocation" (6), a subject that is never far from her own concerns as a writer who constantly inquires into the conditions of her own creativity and who wants to write about being a writer. An enthusiast for literature, Sontag concludes: "A poet's prose is the autobiography of ardor.

All of Tsvetaeva's work is an argument for rapture and for genius, that is, for hierarchy: a poetic of the Promethean" (7)—as is, in its own way, *Under the Sign of Saturn.*

In this first section of *Where the Stress Falls,* Sontag is at her most illuminating when probing and sometimes contesting the reason why certain places at certain times produce great writing, as well as how the writer invests himself in his work. Likening the narrator of Glenway Wescott's neglected classic *The Pilgrim Hawk* to the narrators of other novels that are also disguised versions of writers writing about the failures of writing, Sontag argues: "Tower is describing the vagaries of novel writing as much as the pitfalls of understanding. All these valetudinarian narrators are also writers' self-portraits and exercises in writers' self-mortification" (11).

In the case of Brazilian novelist Machado de Assis, whose narrators write in a sly autobiographical guise, she finds a writer akin to herself, who also exemplifies why Central Europe and Latin America have produced such great prose in the last decades of the twentieth century. Their achievements may not be because of their suffering under "monstrous tyrannies" (32), occasioning a sense of irony and profound seriousness, but rather that they have been more exclusively influenced by the ironic, playful whimsy of Lawrence Sterne's novel *Tristram Shandy,* regarded as a great eccentric work in the English speaking world but also as a profound text for authors who have learned to express themselves through the indirection of the Sternian antihero. Sterne's self-critical protagonist, Sontag suggests, is akin to her own Hippolyte, the narrator of *The Benefactor.* As Sontag reveals: "I thought I was writing a satire on optimism and on certain cherished (by me) ideas of the inner life and of a religiously nourished inwardness" (36).

Like Machado de Assis, an author who is present everywhere in his work and yet cannot be pinned down as to what is truly expressive of his own person, W. G. Sebald seems to write as himself and yet is constructing a narrator other than himself in the author's own voice. Or as Sontag puts it: "Is the narrator Sebald? Or a fictional character to whom the author has lent his name, and selected elements of his biography?" Sebald gives an "effect of the real" (40) by including documents and photographs, and yet, Sontag suspects, this evidence is fabricated, so that the evidence itself becomes a device of the fiction. Echoing her own work in historical fiction, Sontag extols Sebald's "morally accelerated travel narratives—history-minded in their obsessions; fictional in their reach" (43).

In the essay that follows, Sontag notes that Polish novelist Adam Zagajewski writes as though "every life can be construed as embodying exemplary experiences and historical momentousness" (50). That insight is what leads her to deplore culture warriors such as George Steiner, who mourn the "Death of High Culture" in ever more portentous terms, asserting the "superiority of the past over the present" (59). Sontag, accused of retreating from her interest in contemporary popular culture, seems at pains to emphasize that her devotion to great literature is not that of a conservative—that is, she writes not to eulogize but to proselytize, believing there is not only still an audience for masterpieces but also another one in the making.

Sontag tries to prove no negatives in *Where the Stress Falls*. She returns to heroes like Roland Barthes, whose motto is her own: "the exercise of taste . . . means, usually, to praise" (64). She finds Barthes endlessly inventive and defends his use of hyperbole so passionately that it can be read as an endorsement of her own tendency to exaggerate her claims for works of art as a way to dramatize their virtues. She notes Barthes's preference for aphorism (again her own penchant as well) and his partiality to fragments and lists (think of her own "Notes on 'Camp'"). Barthes's willingness to write prefaces to the books of others is, of course, Sontag's own, culminating in her praise of his "wonderful essays on writers" that "must be considered as different versions of his great apologia for the vocation of the writer" (70).

That a writer could simultaneously take ideas so seriously that they become the life of the mind and yet jettison those same ideas is the paradox of literature itself, Sontag implies, in her next essay about *Don Quixote*, which is both about the power of literature and an attack on that power. Cervantes created a character obsessed with what he reads. He represents the writer, who creates his own world in a kind of delirium, which is both destructive and creative.

In "Novel into Film," Sontag returns to one of the themes of *Against Interpretation*—this time commenting on Rainer Werner Fassbinder's *Berlin Alexanderplatz*, a fourteen-part adaptation of Alfred Döblin's novel. She compares this work to Erich von Stroheim's *Greed*, an adaptation of the Frank Norris novel *McTeague*. Sontag suggests that Fassbinder's ruminative and yet theatrical style, as contrasted to von Stroheim's mainly realist visual narration, creates a new kind of cinematic narrative that finally is able to compete with the novel's open form, its ability to digress and yet remain a coherent whole. Even so, she acknowledges that Fassbinder's film is also a tribute to von Stroheim's work, sabotaged by Hollywood standards, which meant the curtailment and, in some cases, the destruction of the director's shooting style and composition.

Sontag's concern with choreography and art fuses in "Grottos: Caves of Mystery and Magic," in which she sees the grotto as "garden art" (134) that transforms space, making it "an elaborately theatric, encrusted space" (136). While such spaces have been commercialized as shopping centers and subway stations, they retain elements of fantasy and excess that Sontag relates to the imagination of horror that is also manifested in the mania for building bomb shelters.

In "A Lexicon for Available Light: Some Notes on Choreography," Sontag describes the development of Lucinda Childs's career, emphasizing the dancer's purity of style, combining elements of classicism and modernism. Childs recapitulated but also reinterpreted the history of dance, using the dance space in a way that is about the love of dance itself. Childs's solo performance in Sontag's film *Unguided Tour,* in which Childs engages in the diagonal postures Sontag praises, mimics the diagonal shots of film that are meant to reflect the dynamic quality of film itself. Similarly, in "Mr. Balanchine," Sontag discusses his classicism in terms of the modernism developed by Isadora Duncan and Mary Wigman. As with her praise of Lucinda Childs, Sontag sees a fruitful set of influences informing both traditional and innovative forms of dance. What matters is the perfection of the art, she concludes, not whether the movement is balletic or anti-balletic.

Sontag's interest in dance, however, goes well beyond her interest in particular dancers or choreographers. She notes in her tribute to Lincoln Kirstein, whom she considers the "finest historian of dance" (184), that "no species of performing artist is as self-critical as a dancer" (187). Dance becomes, in other words, the very epitome of the quest for perfection. In Sontag's experience, no other kind of performing artist takes compliments less seriously or is more eager to point out the flaws in his or her own performance. Dancers are not only cruel to their bodies, usually incurring at least discomfort if not pain, but they also refuse to believe that they can ever be quite worthy of "the god Dance" (188).

It is this transcendent nature of art that also marks Wagner's operas. Quite aside from what his operas say, or what is made of Wagner's ideas—his Romanticism and proto-fascism—is his exploration of the "very nature of love," Sontag suggests in "Wagner's Fluids." What his operas dramatize, and what Wagner devotees can never seem to get enough of, is the portrayal of love as "an emotion always in excess of its object; insatiable." So tragic is this eroticism and exaltation that it "*has* to self-destruct" (202), Sontag concludes. Whereas opera before Wagner centered on the voice, his work orchestrated an "apotheosis of the collective spirit," not through the feats of a singer but by "exhausting, relentlessly ecstatic music" (209).

When Sontag returns to the subject of photography, she recapitulates the arguments of her landmark book but also narrows the focus to the photograph that makes of the past an aesthetic object, as she notes in her preface to a book about one hundred years of Italian photography. Even the subject of prostitution in Bellocq's photographs, which Sontag as a woman simply cannot regard as romantic, nevertheless seems presented in a forthright depiction of women at home, with themselves in a "vanished world" (224) that only the photographs can present with so much charm.

"Certain Mapplethorpes," a memoir/essay about the work of a photographer/friend, is a rare instance of Sontag fusing her subject matter to herself—in this case explaining her reluctance to pose for the camera because it is a pose, a look for which she had become famous, but a look carefully contrived by the photographer. Thus her own collaboration in the confection of, in a sense, a false image—or at best a partial truth—fully implicates herself in the argument she has made elsewhere against the idea that photographs cannot ever, in any simple sense, document reality.

Sontag's other essay on photography, "A Photograph Is Not an Opinion, Or Is It?," originally written as an introduction to Annie Leibovitz's book *Women*, adds little to her earlier commentary on photography and is strangely silent on the style and substance of Leibovitz's own work, as reviewers were quick to note. This reticence is especially striking because Leibovitz was closely associated with Sontag (although Sontag denied they were lovers) and because Leibovitz straddled the line between commercial and high art that surely was worthy of some examination, given Sontag's own rather rueful commentary on the ubiquity of photographs and how they have been taken as dispositive evidence of real events.

"There and Here," the last section of *Where the Stress Falls*, contains some of Sontag's most autobiographical writing, beginning with "Homage to Halliburton," an essay that lovingly reconstructs Sontag's youthful enthusiasm for this world traveler/writer who inspired her own restless spirit and travel writing. His sense of giving himself over to the adventure of writing about travel, which is also an adventure, motivates Sontag and shapes her view of what literature is supposed to be. Just as Halliburton's writing grew out of his travels, Sontag's writing grows out of her love of literature. In "Singleness," she calls herself "literature's servant" (257). She writes, she insists, not to express herself but to contribute to literature, a theme she continues in the next essay, "Writing as Reading."

In "Thirty Years Later," originally a preface to a new edition of *Against Interpretation*, Sontag comments on her youthful desire to combat philistinism and what she calls "aesthetic shallowness" (267). If she wrote more about film than literature in that book, it was because at the time she regarded new movies as more to her taste than new novels. This did not mean, however, that she had abandoned her allegiance to the novel or to other arts in favor of popular culture—as some critics seemed to think.

"Questions of Travel," like "Thirty Years Later," is retrospective insofar as Sontag describes intellectual travelers as seeking alternatives to traditional societies and, in the twentieth century, to capitalist states. So, new socialist governments in Cuba and China seemed to offer an antidote to Western consumerism and predatory capitalism. Revolutionary societies seemed to exemplify a kind of purity and even simplicity lacking in the developed countries. Sontag says little about the extent to which she was implicated in such trips—like her own to Hanoi and to China—even though she admits such carefully staged trips were visits to the "Disneyland of revolution" (281).

"The Idea of Europe (One More Elegy)" is Sontag's especially bitter regret that contemporary Europe has become enveloped in consumerist culture. She is dismayed that the continent that has been for her the treasure house of culture seems bent on a political unification that has "invariably promoted the suppression and erasure of cultural differences, and the concentration and augmentation of state power" (284). Prosperity and liberty are now equated with self-interest and prosperity, she argues, continuing her theme in the next piece, "The Comical Lament of Pyramus and Thisbe" (see chapter six, "Experiments in Theater"). In an even grimmer assessment in "Answers to a Questionnaire," she concludes that in the last twenty years of the twentieth century capitalist countries have discredited the very idea of "idealisms, of altruism itself" (294). To this cynicism she opposes her own role in Sarajevo, a cause Western intellectuals should have embraced—as they did the Spanish Civil War—but did not, as she points out in the next essay, "There and Here." A new kind of philistinism has taken over, she contends, so that her work on a production of *Waiting for Godot* was greeted outside Sarajevo with skepticism and even ridicule (see chapter six, "Experiments in Theater").

Sontag's last two essays, "Joseph Brodsky" and "On Being Translated," are in effect her final effort to emphasize her role as devotee and promoter of a world literature through her own work and through her promotion of figures such as the exiled Russian poet who wrote, as he said, to impress his predecessors, not his contemporaries. His devotion to literature, like Sontag's, expresses the antidote to what Sontag calls "transnational capitalist world culture" (343).

At the Same Time: Essays and Speeches (2007), published posthumously, is a collection Sontag was assembling at the time of her death. As the editors of the volume explain, they have included all the pieces she intended to include, but she did not have the opportunity to revise writing made to order for specific occasions, such as the awards honoring her, and for introductions to literary works she admired by authors foreign to the Anglo-American canon, many of whom were being translated into English for the first time. While the book's title is not Sontag's, the editors suggest that it captures the "polyphonic quality" of prose that treats "politics, aesthetics and ethics, inner and outer life" as inseparable (x). The title is also an apt allusion to the simultaneity of Sontag's concerns. Even in the long period between writing her early and later novels, she never ceased thinking about the composition of fiction, drafting narratives she abandoned or delayed completing. And during her full-time return to fiction she could not resist returning to the subjects of earlier essay volumes, even as she wrote and directed plays and films.

At the Same Time begins brilliantly with "An Argument About Beauty," an essay that recalls her anatomy of vital cultural terms in Against Interpretation and Styles of Radical Will. Typical of her sly sallies, she defines beauty as a term signifying an "indisputable excellence," and then in the same sentence notes that, as such, the word has been employed as a "perennial resource in the issuing of peremptory evaluations" (1). So it is that Sontag seizes on how one word can exemplify the tyranny of taste and carry with it a moral and aesthetic authority. Right from the start, she overturns her early work, which favors the separation of aesthetics and morality, as Oscar Wilde, a major influence on her, tended to do.

Also on display is a historical consciousness heightened because of Sontag's devotion to re-creating the past in The Volcano Lover and In America. Relying on beauty to enforce aesthetic standards and good taste is not feasible, she contends, because the very idea of discrimination (meaning the ability to judge value) has been attenuated in a social and political order that is no longer based on exclusion as defined by "station, class, hierarchy" (6). Who has the right, in other words, to rank excellence?

Sontag provides no antidote to the diminishing authority that at one time secured some consensus about the beautiful and hence the worthwhile works of art and the worldviews they embody—except to offer, indirectly, her own experience as the only kind of wisdom now capable of enjoining a bond between aesthetics and morality. Who else can she be thinking of when she writes, "And the wisdom that becomes available over a deep, lifelong engagement with the aesthetic cannot, I venture to say, be duplicated by any other kind of seriousness" (9)? In short, this lead essay is her bid to command the reader's assent to her unique authority, a mastery that in fact led to the awards that became the occasions of the prose pronouncements in this volume.

The next four essays, dealing with the lives and works of Pasternak, Tsvetaeva, Rilke, Dostoevsky, Anna Banti, and Victor Serge, recall the methods of Under the Sign of Saturn, in which Sontag fuses the writer's character with his or her work. In the first of these appreciations, Rilke becomes a cynosure around which other important writers organize their careers. Like the role the Russian poet Joseph Brodsky played in Sontag's own life, Rilke exemplifies the highest standards of literature and seriousness. In her view, figures such as Rilke have an extraliterary quality, in that they not only inspire the making of art but also appear, in her reverent prose, as the equivalent of saints, exalted figures worthy of worship, and intercessors for the perpetuation of the highest literature.

It is not surprising, then, that she elevates Leonid Tsypkin, a doctor, into her pantheon. Tsypkin eked out a living in the Stalinist Soviet Union, purposely eschewing the literary life both out of a desire to avoid government persecution and also out of an immaculate sense of literature that did not truckle with the coercive practices of literary establishments. For all her own literary establishmentarianism, Sontag continued to admire outsiders who single-mindedly pursue their art—in this case devoting years to what she calls "parafiction" (19), a re-creation of Dostoevsky's life in *Summer in Baden-Baden*. Her account of the novel's way of proceeding could serve just as well as an account of *The Volcano Lover:* "a retelling of the life of a real person of accomplishment from another era, it interweaves this story with a story in the present, the novelist mulling over, trying to gain deeper entry into the inner life of someone whose destiny it was to have become not only historical but monumental" (29).

For Sontag, writing about literature and literary figures is always aspiring to be in itself a work of literature, although the Sontag of the 1960s would not have acknowledged what turned her essay writing into novels: an awareness of history as it impinges on a writer who as part of that awareness is compelled to write about that history and to change it. Anna Banti makes the novelist's consciousness central when re-creating history, and thus she provides Sontag with an example of how the historical novel can be much more than just a record of fact, even when it is informed by documents and research. In effect, Banti demonstrates how the writer can impose upon history (40). The novelist is always sovereign, Sontag insists, even when her material is history. Indeed, she wraps historical fiction in a kind of mystique, insisting that to "write well about the past is to write something like fantastic fiction. It is the strangeness of the past, rendered with piercing concreteness, that gives the effect of realism" (52). The novelist who nearly swamps *In America* with detailed data from the past while picturing herself in a room with her characters suffuses these late-period literary essays, paradoxically touting the supremacy of the imagination even as she is claiming to render a real past—not a fantasy—even if the effect is fantastic.

Sontag was well aware that her own turn to historical fiction would be regarded in some quarters as a retreat from her avant-garde essays of the 1960s, when narrative itself became suspect and the ordering of events into a realistic pattern was renounced. Banti's achievement, Sontag argues, is characteristic of historical novels that have become original contributions to twentieth century literature (53). This contention turns the modernism Sontag touted in her earliest essays on its head. Joyce and Faulkner, even when setting their work in the past, deliberately avoided, in the main, the tropes and conventions of historical novels, suggesting that to submit to history, to the historical record, meant the subservience of art to documentation. She is on sounder ground when she suggests that the "dialogical voice, which set a story in the past in order to dwell on its relation to the present [is] very much a modern project" (53). She might as well be describing a novel like *Absalom, Absalom!* with its accompaniment of argumentative narrators.

The fourth essay in *At the Same Time,* "The Case for Victor Serge," is perfectly positioned to transition to Sontag's role as political polemicist. Like the preceding essays, this exercise in appreciation of a nearly forgotten writer features her powerful ability to evoke a writer's oeuvre and accomplishment. Serge was an example of an activist writer, a Russian revolutionary who bravely criticized the revolution, endured imprisonment, and never abandoned his idea of a just revolution simply to side with his fellow Communists. His novels, Sontag suggests, are not so much reflections of his personal experience as they are transformations of his understanding of history into powerful plots and characters. His fiction creates a truth that no faithful rendering of history can rival, she avows. Instead of the elegiac and regretful tones of ex-Communists who exhibit the "requisite tones of despair or contrition or bewilderment," he was indomitable and unsparing in his truth telling. "Because he was right, he has been punished as a writer of fiction," (61) Sontag concludes.

How can Sontag be so sure of that judgment? She does not say but again seems to be writing out of her own experience, when she stood up in 1982 and publicly repudiated her former Communist affiliations, and without much regret or direct self-criticism. It was a stance that infuriated many on the left who had soldiered with her in Communist causes. It does not seem too much to say that in Serge's plight she read her own. Even as she explains why Serge stood out from his Communist confreres, she is examining her own delayed reckoning with her enthusiasms for revolutions in China and Cuba. Because writers on the left were appalled at the prospect of a third world war, they were loathe to single out the Soviet Union and treat it as the sole enemy, she argues. What is more, she asserts, anti-Communism was too often associated with anti-Semitism and racism, and therefore, siding with anti-Communists meant endorsing reactionary politics.

But Sontag's explanation of this period is seriously skewed, since she respects only the anti-Communism of her cherished *Partisan Review* and the testimony of Polish poet Czeslaw Miłosz who saw firsthand the tyranny of his country's Communist leaders but was dismissed by many on the left as a Cold

War propagandist. Robert Conquest also gets an honorable mention as first exposing the Soviet Gulag. But to suggest that these voices were the only—or even the most prominent—writers who offered an alternative to reactionary anti-Communism is at once to distort the multi-vocal opposition to Communism and to elide Sontag's own inability to comprehend it. Nowhere is Orwell or Rebecca West or Raymond Aron mentioned in Sontag's book, and yet their views (coming from the left) are crucial to an understanding of Serge's place in the literature of anti-Communism. Unlike Serge, however, West, Orwell, and Aron, while attracted to socialism, were never true believers in Communism to begin with. In other words, they did not experience the disillusionment of former Communists that makes Serge so attractive to Sontag. To write about Aron, Orwell, or West, especially, would have opened up a range of choices that those on the left, including Sontag, deliberately rejected for decades. Instead, Sontag takes refuge in suggesting that those who were reluctant or even refused to criticize the Soviet Union had meant well (73), even though she does not say that the good intentions helped justify the tyrannies she would belatedly denounce.

Sontag did not live long enough to perhaps enlarge the historical perspective of her essay on Serge. Its position in *At the Same Time* is apposite and yet abrupt, considering that "Outlandish," the next piece extolling Halldor Laxness's novel *Under the Glacier,* is an amusing and profound send-up of the realistic novel, which seems oddly out of place since it recurs to the themes of the essays that come before her appreciation of Serge. And even more disconcerting is the next set of essays dealing with 9/11, a grouping of commentaries that seriously undermines the authoritative voice that the first part of *At the Same Time* establishes so powerfully.

Sontag's initial response to the attack provoked considerable controversy, especially since her opening words make it sound as though America had it coming. It had been given a "monstrous dose of reality." In effect, her first inclination was to condemn American ignorance and the rhetoric of government officials and the media that spoke of a "cowardly" attack on "civilization," instead of acknowledging an "attack on the world's self-proclaimed superpower, undertaken as a consequence of specific American alliances and actions" (103). As in many of her earlier political polemics, Sontag engaged in name-calling and epithets about a "robotic president" and his "reality-concealing rhetoric" (104). What is entirely missing from her first response, as she concedes in a second piece, was a simple and sincere reaction to the sudden and devastating loss of life. Instead, she chose to disparage the media's "confidence-building language" and "psychotherapy" (105) that obscured the root causes of the attack.

Sontag had been in Berlin watching on television the disintegration of the World Trade Center towers. A week later she returned to New York City to get as near as possible to the site of devastation, she writes in "A Few Weeks After." This was as close as she could come to recanting her first reaction to the attack: "In those first days after my return to New York, the reality of the devastation, and the immensity of the loss of life, made my initial focus on the rhetoric surrounding the event seem to me less relevant." Her essay seems unaware of the irony of using the words "the reality of the devastation," when her earlier reaction had suggested she knew what the reality was and most Americans did not. Now she begins not with a speech about a "monstrous reality" hitting an oblivious country but rather about "an appalling crime." In an extraordinary reversal of her first response, she rejects the view that "America has brought this horror upon itself" (111). But this is surely the implication of her first response.

Like *Where the Stress Falls, At the Same Time* begins at this point to look like an inchoate miscellany, with brilliant essays chucked between reiterations of previous work, such as "Photography: A Summa." Of more consequence are such pieces as "Regarding the Torture of Others," in which she shows how the rhetoric and politics of the American government inescapably led to torture and contraventions of international law that culminated in the humiliation of prisoners at Abu Ghraib, the torture center established by Saddam Hussein. As Sontag observes, what is most disturbing about the photographs coming out of that prison were the unmistakable signs that prisoner abuse was viewed as a form of entertainment. And just as bad were those in the American media who excused the Abu Ghraib atrocities as simply a way to blow off steam. That certain American congressmen were more concerned about how America's reputation suffered than about the abuses themselves convinces Sontag that violation of decent human standards and law had become routine, so that soldiers posed in celebration of torture, taking pictures as souvenirs. And why not? she suggests, since it is now commonplace to expose private lives and to reveal all on television.

Sontag connects the moment with history, the appalling Abu Ghraib, with a disregard for fundamental human decencies that is now pervasive in American culture. She does much the same abroad, arguing in "The Conscience of Words," her Jerusalem Prize acceptance speech, that the "doctrine of collective responsibility, as a rationale for collective punishment, is never justified, militarily or ethically" (150). Thus to bomb and otherwise terrorize civilians in territory where "hostile military activity" occurs is wrong. She is, of course, criticizing Israel for creating flashpoints of conflict that have resulted in loss of civilians' lives. The policy of establishing settlements in the occupied territories has to be stopped and reversed, and the military presence supporting those settlements has to be withdrawn if peace is to be restored to the region (150).

Also on display in *At the Same Time* is Sontag's remarkable grasp of how literature relates to the other arts. In "The World as India: The St. Jerome Lecture on Literary Translation," she observes: "Dancers are trained to strive for the not entirely chimerical goal of perfection: exemplary, error-free expressiveness. In a literary translation, given the multiple imperatives to which a literary translation has to respond, there can only be a superior, never a perfect, performance." If the proper way to approach translation vexes her, it is, in part, because she laments the decline in the number of great foreign works that are no longer translated into English and do not appear in the American market, or appear but do not generate the kinds of significant sales that important European and South American writers used to enjoy in the United States.

An elegiac tone suffuses *At the Same Time,* as Sontag continues to tout great works of literature while acknowledging their disappearance from the language of public discourse. Above all, she resolutely seeks readers to perpetuate the modern canon because, as she puts it in "Literature Is Freedom," "One task of literature is to formulate questions and construct counterstatements to the reigning pieties" (202). Art is not always oppositional, she concedes, and yet it is as a dissenter that she stakes her own claims to the reader's attention. As with nearly all of Sontag's work, her abiding interest is in stimulating an argument, a dialogue that is the lifeblood of literature and what she struggled to live for, always.

Reviewers, in the main, treated *At the Same Time* respectfully—if also noting that her literary essays were far more nuanced than her political ones. Even critics like Robert Boyers, one of Sontag's most sympathetic readers, noticed how the collection continued with her curious combination of formal argument and "reckless assertiveness."[4] Boyers pounced on her pomposity, quoting and then setting aside her judgments—such as her pronouncement that Laxness's *Under the Glacier* is "'a work of supreme derision and wit.' Supreme. 'It is one of the funniest books ever written.' Ever." In spite of her lofty and extravagant phrase making, Boyers praised her deep absorption in her subjects and her desire to test the limits of her arguments. Many of the reviews, naturally enough, took the form of tributes for a writer so recently deceased and so necessary to the arena of cultural debate that she did so much to foster.

CHAPTER 8

The Diaries

In the preface to the first volume of his mother's diaries, David Rieff admits he cannot say whether or not his mother wanted her diaries to be published. The first volume, *Reborn,* represents Rieff's selection of entries from 1947 to 1963. He cannot know, he notes, what entries she would have published, if any. And she left no instructions about her diaries, her uncollected writings, her papers, and her unfinished work. But she sold her papers (manuscripts, notebooks, letters to and from her, and e-mails) to the University of California at Los Angeles with no restrictions, although the material that will make up the third volume of diaries has been held back until that volume is published and, presumably, until her authorized biographer, Benjamin Moser, completes his work. It seems reasonable to conclude, however, that since Sontag chose to preserve her papers in a university archive, she realized that someday the diaries and her other unpublished writing would be available on some basis to scholars and most likely to the public. Whether the UCLA archive represents all of Sontag's literary estate is not clear, especially since an undetermined amount of material seems to have been removed from her e-mail folders before being sent to UCLA.[1] Many of those folders are now empty. Rieff makes no mention of his mother destroying any of her papers. She expected to recover from her third cancer and did not realize she would die until the last few weeks of her life.

Rieff believes that his mother wrote her diaries for herself since she never published anything from them and never shared them with friends, although, as Rieff admits, friends were aware of her notebooks, which she kept among photographs and other private possessions. And yet Sontag's own literary consciousness was first formed by her teenage reading of André Gide's journals. And so it is difficult to believe that she did not, on some level, think of posterity in leaving behind a very intense and detailed record of her life. Rieff remembers his mother making only one cryptic reference to the diaries—a "single whispered sentence: 'You know where the diaries are'" (ix). They constitute a conversation with herself, which is part of their great value, since she was able to express certain ideas and emotions that never appeared in her interviews and, in some cases, not even in the conversations she had with her son and her friends and lovers. If she left no instructions as to the disposal of her diaries or publication, it is perhaps because they were a part of her private self so long as she could breathe that one sentence.

The sheer volume of notebooks—close to a hundred, Rieff reports—makes it even more difficult to believe that she was not amassing what is virtually the alternative canonical version of her work, the version that did not get vetted, edited, or otherwise mediated through the formal process of publishing. That she did not tamper with her diaries or prepare them for publication does not, however, mean that they are necessarily more honest or reliable than her published work. And yet her reflections on herself, her sexuality, her family and friends, certainly shows sides of Sontag that would otherwise be occluded, if not erased from her biography. And these diaries, read beside her letters and e-mails, as well as the letters written to her, open up new ways of exploring the origins of her work. So far, however, no plans have been announced for a collection of letters from or to her.

Rieff presents himself as his mother's reluctant editor, deciding to proceed with publication because of the existence of her archive. If he did not organize and publish the diaries, at some point someone else would, he notes. But that someone else could not have proceeded without Rieff's permission, and although he claims not to have restricted anything important in his mother's diaries, a conflict of interest remains. As valuable at the diaries are, they should also be used in the full knowledge that a family member has edited them—not exactly the sort of scholarly procedure that modern readers have come to expect in the handling of an author's unpublished materials.

That Rieff has, however, acted in contravention of his mother's own behavior during her lifetime is undeniable. As he admits, his mother was not a "self-revealing person. . . . She avoided to the extent she could, without denying it, her own homosexuality or any acknowledgment of her ambition" (ix). And yet why Rieff refers to one of Sontag's lovers as "H," rather than giving her full name is bizarre, since Harriet Sohmers agreed to be interviewed and her name was freely used in the 2000 publication of *Susan Sontag: The Making of an Icon*. Other names of real individuals are also omitted, although Rieff's reasons for disguising some names and not others is not divulged.

Rieff is right to stress the almost Victorian earnestness of Sontag's journal. He aptly compares her to Thomas Carlyle, the author of *Heroes and Hero*

Worship, which could easily have been the title of one of Sontag's books. Even so, Rieff is right to say that there is also something very American about Susan Sontag in her desire for rebirth and new beginnings, a desire that dominates her diaries. That the diaries are also a record of disappointed love, of the conflicting role of Eros in her life, "makes me sadder than I can possibly convey," (xii) Rieff laments. It is important to know that, as he puts it, she was as "uncomfortable with her body as she was serene about her mind" (xii). She was always praising the sensual in art and yet found it so lacking in her own experience, although the list of her lovers in the diaries would seem to contradict her seemingly too-earnest evaluation of her love affairs. Perhaps the greatest irony in the diaries is that they are about the very ambitions Sontag was so loathe to acknowledge when questioned about them. In the end, Rieff seems to give himself and readers permission to read the diaries, since he concludes by emphasizing how much his mother loved to read diaries, "the more intimate the better" (xiv). So, he supposes, she might approve of what he has done. What he does not say is that the diaries also reflect (although not enough) how much Sontag reveled in gossip, in what was happening not only to those close to her but also to those she considered her rivals. Thus these diaries are, in a way, yet another bid to have the last word.

Dated November 23, 1947, Sontag's first diary entry is a declaration of principles in the form of a list from a to h. She declared that she was no believer in a "personal god" (1) or in the immortality of the soul. She took an Emersonian position on being true to herself as the best form of honesty. She believed that human beings differ only in intelligence. She sounded like a utilitarian when she announced that the happiness of the individual should be the cause for action. It is wrong to take a human life, she stated, making no exceptions. Already, her politics were those of the socialist who believed in a strong central government in control of public utilities, banks, mines, and transportation. Such a government would support the arts, guarantee a minimum wage, provide for the disabled, the aged, and pregnant women regardless of their marital status.

The nascent Susan Sontag also emerges in her April 13, 1948, entry: "Ideas disturb the levelness of life" (1). The statement seems born out of her impatience with what she deemed southern California blandness and conformity but also represents a sensibility keen to argue her ideas, which she hoped would move the world to other, higher levels. But the adolescent Sontag feared she might give in to her mother, who wanted her to remain at home while attending college. Her mother's sorrow made Sontag feel cruel, but at the same time she retreated to her room to play a Mozart opera and fortify her desire to be on her own. Such entries demonstrate how much willpower it took for Sontag to break from her family, and these early declarations also underscore what becomes a dominant theme in her work: the strength of the will, which Maryna Zaleska in *In America,* for example, dwells on as she embarks on reshaping her life by moving from Poland to the United States.

André Gide became Sontag's indispensable guide, as she noted on September 10, 1948, after her first reading of his journals. She finished reading the book at 2:30 A.M. on the same day she had purchased it. She immediately decided that she must reread the volume more slowly a second time. She treated Gide as her liberator, but she also saw the book as a projection of herself, as if she had created it. On December 19, 1948, Sontag began the first of many reading lists that she would include in her diaries. On the list are several Gide titles, Sherwood Anderson's *Tar,* and William Faulkner's *Sanctuary,* as well as titles by English and European writers such as George Moore and Dostoyevsky. Her leftist politics are apparent in her reading of Dalton Trumbo's antiwar novel *Johnny Got His Gun.* She was already reading classics by Dante, Ariosto, Pushkin, and Rimbaud, and she included several dramatists such as O'Neill, Shaw, Calderón, and Hellman. David Rieff notes that this list is more than five pages long and has more than one hundred titles. Already Sontag was thinking of art not only in terms of its content but its form, noting that language is "not only an instrument but an end in itself" (7). She was drawn to music because of its purity of form and sensuality. The mindset of *Against Interpretation* is apparent in these incipient meditations on art.

In her December 25, 1948, entry, Sontag alluded to her "lesbian tendencies" (9). By April 6, 1949, she lamented her inability to make love to a man. She felt degraded when she kissed him. Tellingly, she exclaimed that she wanted to hide, a decision she would stick by until nearly the end of her life, when it then became impossible to deflect interest in her sexuality because it had become a part of her biography.

By the end of 1948, Sontag had established a tone for her diaries that would remain consistent even as she matured: an intense disappointment in herself that seemed to arise out of her high expectations and aspirations. She acknowledged a masochistic streak and a divided sensibility, wishing to stay in the comfort of home but realizing she must leave in order to grow intellectually. She said as much when she noted on February 11, 1949, her agreement to attend Berkeley. There she seemed no happier, and in a mood almost of resignation she identified university teaching as the only profession that appealed to her. David Rieff notes that she later added a one-word comment: "Jesus!" Yet the studious, graduate school–like quality of her desire to amass knowledge and collect it in lists and books and her encyclopedic references to authors and ideas suggest a mind that never quite transcended its academic roots. Indeed, her diaries reveal her as a kind of transitional figure occupying places in both higher education and in the world of artists and an intellectually engaged public.

However unsatisfying Sontag's semester at Berkeley, it served the purpose of finally breaking forever the hold of home on her. She spent a weekend with her mother and realized that she was ready to leave this small world and that she would no longer be dependent on her mother for emotional sustenance. At several crucial moments in Sontag's life—her Berkeley semester, her two years at the University of Chicago, her decision to study at Oxford, her move to New York—changes of location proved essential in the next stage of her development as a person and writer. The impact of these moves had its ultimate impact on her work in *In America,* where Maryna Zaleska cannot conceive of a new self unless she leaves her native Poland, and she cannot conceive of America as other than a stage on which to perform her new self. Similarly, Sontag's reading of Goethe's *Sorrows of Young Werther,* mentioned in a May 17, 1949, entry, would have its exhilarating denouement in the passages about the Cavaliere's wife, Catherine, whose sedate life is suddenly disrupted but also fulfilled by her reading of the famous bildungsroman.

Sontag's own coming of age occurred in San Francisco, where she toured the gay bars with Harriet Sohmers, a Berkeley student who initiated Sontag into a lesbian life. Sontag recorded how little she knew then by describing her admiration for a beautiful blond singer with a powerful voice. A smiling Harriet had to tell Susan that the singer was a man. In this part of the diaries Sontag described sex and making love with a directness absent from her fiction, let alone her essays. Sex was a difficult subject for her to handle in print, as her son David Rieff suggests, and her own experience, especially at first, was tentative, and she described herself in the act of making love as "stiff." But the understanding she came to in the act of love she underlined: *"I knew everything then, nor have I forgotten it now"* (25). This avowal is part of what David Rieff identifies as almost thirty pages of Sontag's account of her life in Berkeley, an entry begun on May 23, 1949. How much of this account Rieff left out is impossible to determine. But it is clear that Sontag was excited by overcoming what she called the "agonized dichotomy between the body and the mind that has had me on the rack for the past two years" (18). In fact, after her experience with Harriet, Sontag declared her desire to have many love affairs. In her published work, her interest in sex seemed displaced in essays on pornography and on the Marquis de Sade, in which she maintained a cool, reserved, intellectual discussion of the subject. But these essays also have deep roots in Sontag's exploration of the language of sex and sexual identity. By August 3, 1949, she was compiling a list of gay slang, including words such as *swish* (effeminate) and *chippie* (a one-night stand with a woman), and contrasting heterosexual

words and phrases such as *box* for vagina and *get a piece of tail* (a male having sexual intercourse with a woman). If Sontag was wary of being more open
about her sexuality, she may have had in mind what she noted in her diary for
August 5, 1949. Some friends had said: Date men. Otherwise it would be too
late to reverse her preference for women.

Sontag's comments on lectures at Berkeley sized up the faculty, with courses
like *The Age of Johnson* stimulating her, and others that seemed merely com-
petently presented but without much originality. Already she was concerned
about "letting myself slide into the academic life" (6). Her tastes were already
avant-garde, and she rejected the English Department's stultifying publications
such as "The Social Criticism of Fenimore Cooper" and "A Bibliography of
the Writings of Bret Harte in the Magazines and Newspapers of California
(1859–1891)." Her disgust with the staid university world is set against the
backdrop of Harriet's announcing to her friends that she is going to "rescue"
Susan.

Sontag appears in the diaries as, in her own estimation, a naïf, but also as a
self-conscious student of her own youth, remarking wryly on August 26, 1949,
that she was entering the "anarchist-aesthete phase of my youth" (44). She read
I. A. Richards's *Practical Criticism* and Arthur Koestler's anti-Stalinist novel
Darkness at Noon. But the issues of her sexuality continued to engage her.
When she arrived for her first semester at the University of Chicago, she found
in a bookstore on State Street copies of Wilhelm Stekel's *The Homosexual
Neurosis* and *Bisexual Love*. She noted Stekel's belief that humans are naturally
bisexual, although only the Greeks understood that to be the case.

Although she would not settle in New York until the end of the 1950s, Sontag was already making excursions to visit museums and attend plays, including *Death of a Salesman* and *The Madwoman of Chaillot*. She was an astute
student of both staging and acting, and she was already trying to work out
how art should be described. It gave pleasure but how could that be measured?
At this point, she did not have an answer. Then, on November 11, 1949, she
reported that she had been given a splendid job as a researcher for sociology
instructor Philip Rieff. Now she would be able to concentrate "in one area with
competent guidance" (54). How she moved from this excited but hardly passionate entry to marrying Rieff less than two weeks later remains a mystery in
the diaries, except insofar as her writing to herself reveals a sensibility yearning
for an overwhelming commitment to a life of ideas and of passion, and that no
one, until Rieff, seemed in a position to provide stability and the guidance.

At the end of 1949, Sontag, back in California for the holidays, visited
Thomas Mann, an event that she put a year earlier in her memoir, "Pilgrimage," perhaps to obviate the need to deal with the connection to Rieff and

also, apparently, to intensify her role, once again, as intellectual naïf bearding the master artist in his den. The diary account is more prosaic and lacks the sardonic retrospective tone of "Pilgrimage." She quoted his comments on *The Magic Mountain,* which he meant, he said, as a "summa" (55) on the period leading up to World War I. The meeting was something of a disappointment because Mann's remarks could not match the eloquence of his novel. It seems that this crucial meeting with a literary hero convinced Sontag that it was better to know the art than the artist. But Sontag also seems to have been fascinated with Mann's comments on James Joyce and Proust, which may have been instigated by her. What Sontag thought of her encounter with Mann, then, is hard to say, except to note that she left with no particular insight, no epiphany, which thus left room for the anticlimactic ambiance of "Pilgrimage." That she was looking for some kind of denouement, however risky, seems apparent in her cryptic entry for January 3, 1951, in which she announced her marriage to Rieff, fearful of her "will toward self-destructiveness" (62).[2]

Marriage did not change Sontag's two-year trajectory at the University of Chicago, where she spent heady semesters in philosophy and literature courses, absorbing the ideas and manners of famed professors such as Elder Olson, R. S. Crane, Leo Strauss, and Kenneth Burke. And yet, as she noted in her entry for November 12, 1950, she remained a disciple of Jack London's novel *Martin Eden,* the story of a writer who commits suicide (Sontag understood the oddness of her inspiration) but one that nonetheless expressed her attraction to the sheer energy of creativity.

Entries for the years 1950–1955 are sparse, and David Rieff cannot say whether the notebooks were lost or whether his mother wrote no more than he found. What she thought in those early years of her marriage, and how those early years shaped her intellectual outlook, can only be pieced together from her later writings, which, of course, are memories rendered into the fiction of *I, etcetera* and *In America,* which may well distort as much as they reveal about the true nature of her marriage. Of more concern to her in the extant entries was her son, David, whom she loved to observe, noting the child's self-absorbed nature in entries for August 17, 1954, and September 4, 1956.

In late 1956, Sontag dwelt on marriage as a torment, a way of subduing feelings in a life of mutual dependency. Arguments that have no satisfactory conclusion bothered her, and she admitted that after the marriage's first year, the urge to reconcile had atrophied into angry silences that gradually gave way to relations as usual. She later called this state "inertia" (84). Some of the silences and hostilities of marriage are evident in *Duet for Cannibals,* especially in that film's evocation of the claustrophobic nature of marriage. In her diary, Sontag noted Rilke's belief that marriage is sustainable only through continuing separations and returns. As Sontag would later say, Rieff remained at her side always, continuing conversations even when she went to the bathroom.

Throughout the end of 1956, conversations with David seemed to buoy her, and she enjoyed talking with him about the nature of God, of death, and of the new words he was learning to use, such as *sarcophagus* and *esophagus* (90). But as she noted on January 3, 1957: "the sense of not being free has never left me these six years" (96). She referred to the "leakage of talk" (87), apparently meaning nothing said was of any consequence.

On January 6, 1957, Sontag complained about her "flabby" (90) will. This would in her later writing about Cioran and others, and then in *In America,* become of paramount importance. Her notes on marriage contain more complaints about quarrels and her writer's block. She had ideas for stories but nothing seemed to jell. Perhaps as part of priming her for writing, she set down notes about her childhood, somewhat in the manner of "Project for a Trip to China." Brief glimpses of her life in New York, Tucson, and Miami are listed rather than developed, but the roots of her radicalism are evident in her mentioning a paper she did on the California robber barons for her favorite teacher, Mr. Shepro at North Hollywood High School. She referred to her father, his singing "She'll be comin' 'round the mountain when she comes" (112). She dreamed of the Lone Ranger coming to rescue her from high school and also listening to a speech by John Howard Lawson, a blacklisted screenwriter. She mentioned writing a book on Russia, an assignment for a high school class that she preserved and is now in her UCLA collection. She wept when Franklin Roosevelt died. She told her mother that she would rather not be Jewish—perhaps in reaction to certain insults and after being hit on the head with a rock, an event her sister recalls in the documentary *Regarding Susan Sontag.* Sontag mentioned being called a "kike" at her middle school in Tucson (125).

Sontag's conflicted sexuality is alluded to in her brief mention of threatening to cut her breasts off because she did not want to be a girl when she grew up. She mentioned a journal she began in Tucson (evidently lost or destroyed) with an entry about a dead, rotting dog. These are just flashes of memory—like collecting Classic Comics when she was in the eighth grade. But the memories were apparently fitful and were of a piece with Sontag's reluctance to revisit her childhood and adolescent years by constructing an extended narrative. Instead she was beset by the duties of marriage and childrearing. It was in this context that she exclaimed: "If only I get the fellowship to Oxford!" It would be her chance to escape the "feathered nest" (126). She seemed, to herself, inauthentic. She played Dorothea to Rieff's Casaubon, the dry-as-dust scholar who spends a futile life compiling "A Key to All Mythologies." The diary establishes that

Sontag saw the parallel between her life and George Eliot's novel *Middlemarch* decades before she put it in her novel *In America*. Like Dorothea, Sontag dreaded the loss of her personality. In her lists of do's and don'ts she reminded herself to shower every other night and write her mother every other day. Was there a connection between the dutiful daughter and the wife who was struggling to maintain her mental and physical hygiene in a failing marriage?

On March 19, 1957, Sontag recorded that she had obtained her Oxford fellowship. Philip Rieff seemed devastated; "an ejaculation of weeping" (137) was her terse description. She suffered from migraines and prepared to depart, never really having had a full conversation with her husband. As David Rieff notes (146), Sontag's last day in Cambridge, where she had been studying philosophy and literature at Harvard while Rieff taught at Brandeis, was, in effect, the last day of her marriage. Seeing her off was her Harvard mentor, Jacob Taubes, whose influence on her early writing was significant, especially in her essay about Simone Weil, although Sontag's published work avoids the theological issues she explored in her teaching at Columbia University under Taubes's supervision. If Sontag had pursued an academic career, the philosophy of religion might well have been her specialization. Her course work at Harvard reveals deep engagement with the history of religion, and she excelled in anatomizing various belief systems; this work formed the deep background of her handling of Western culture in *Against Interpretation*.

Although Sontag studied at Oxford, neither its environs nor its curriculum seemed to absorb her. Instead, she went to Italy and then to France in November 1957, visiting churches and galleries and storing up perceptions that would later inform her writing about art in her essays. It is also clear from diary entries that her interests were shifting to bohemianism. Already, she was concerned with philistinism, a deliberate turning away, in her view, from any original or unconventional thinking about art. Rather than philosophers, she was reading Dostoyevsky and D. H. Lawrence. What she thought of her philosophy courses is unfortunately unavailable because David Rieff decided not to include her extensive notes on lectures in the book publication of her diaries.

Sontag reported that Saint-Germain-des-Pres was "not the same as Greenwich Village, exactly" (158), which was the beginning of her exposure not just to European thinkers and culture but to a mode of living and writing that she first read about in André Gide and that she associated with Djuna Barnes's novel *Nightwood,* which had been the subject of her thesis at the University of Chicago. Slowly, Sontag was transforming herself from the philosopher to the artist, and from the academic to the public, independent intellectual. She had not cut her ties to academe, but she was already estranged from the regimen of higher education and moving toward what she called the "café routine"

(158): writing, then meeting with fellow artists in as many as four cafés in one evening. This sampling of shifting cultural milieus became a habit she would pursue in New York City as well, influencing a writing style that was constantly inflected with allusions to various schools of thought, aesthetics, and ethics, as if these ideas were arranged on so many tables to be savored. The Susan Sontag essay that is, in effect, a menu of thought had its origins in her early exposure to Parisian intellectual life.

The first mention of camp occurs in an undated entry (probably made in December 1957). Sontag met Elliot Stein, a New Yorker who wrote for *Opera*, a London publication. His taste for movies like *King Kong* and many of his opinions and insights would eventually be assimilated in "Notes on 'Camp.'" Sontag also met Beat poets and other writers such as Allen Ginsberg and Peter Orlovsky. She resumed relations with Harriet Sohmers, who had seduced Sontag at Berkeley. Sontag now called her the "finest flower of American bohemia" (160). It was a conflicted relationship, with Sontag's having to deal with her sexual longing and Sohmers with her sexual dissatisfactions, as Sontag put it in her diary entry for December 30, 1957. What seems at stake in Sontag's copious diary entries about her relationship with Harriet is how sex becomes intertwined with power—that is, with who is in charge, who leads, and who ultimately determines what the love affair means. This tortured presentation of love is replicated in Sontag's first film, *Duet for Cannibals,* and in *Unguided Tour,* starring Sontag's lover Lucinda Childs.

During Sontag's sojourn in Paris, she began to make extensive notes on films, collecting a range of references that would later be displayed in her essays. She called movies novels in motion (164). She also reflected on her journal keeping, noting that she was not merely recording what happened to her, or expressing her thought and emotions. Instead the journals are an act of self-invention. Sontag used the journals as a project, a construct. When she read Harriet's journal, which confirmed Harriet's dislike of Sontag, Sontag was hurt but also took the occasion to comment again on the purpose of diaries, which were precisely to be read "furtively" (161) by others. In short, more than self-invention is involved in these diaries. They are meant to be read, although Sontag at this point only wondered if Harriet would ever read Sontag's diaries.

Sontag now saw her life in terms of her writing, whereas with Philip Rieff their long conversations seemed only an extension of their intense marriage, which did not get written down in diary form because it was not, in effect, part of Sontag's self-creation. She felt imprisoned by the marriage and, in turn, her writing suffered—indeed was almost extinguished. However unhappy Sontag was with Sohmers, both sought a creative self—what both Hippolyte and Diddy dream of in *The Benefactor* and *Death Kit.*

Sontag's attraction to extremist writers such as Simone Weil, Antonin Artaud, and Jean Genet is explicable in terms of her early struggles in Paris. She felt left out of the bohemian mix that Harriet Sohmers so easily absorbed. Sontag told herself that she was not egotistical enough. She was too timid, too sane, too prudent. She wanted to be more daring and even reckless, as Harriet had no trouble doing. All the same, this tension between Sontag's cautious and wild sides shaped her identity as a writer. Her essays extol the bohemian, but they also tend to preserve an academic decorum. She was a great sampler of bohemianism, but she was not a regular, so to speak. And it was precisely her straddling different worlds that would make her so appealing as a writer about cultural trends (a word she would have despised) who denied that she was trendy. Her slightly removed stance as a narrator of what she saw, read, heard, and analyzed separated her from the phenomena she was nevertheless associated with.

In a fictionalized account of her marriage breakup that is included in her diary, Sontag rejected the "tense careerism of the academic world" (169) and sought the spontaneity and independence that she associated in her essays with the artist's life. And that life consisted not of self-expression but of creating something new. When she considered why people create masks, she suggested in her own case that it was not because she was hiding her true self but rather that she was projecting an identity that is aspirational—what she wanted to become. This comment on herself is of a piece with her essays arguing that the artist's work is not to be understood in autobiographical terms but that it is the form—or the mask, in a sense, the surface of the art—that has to be contemplated, not some hidden meaning to be excavated. So she counseled herself not to look for shapes and scenes in abstract painting but instead to appreciate their plasticity.

To be an artist, to be a person, for Sontag, was to have a sense of vocation—a point she made when criticizing Harriet for behaving like no more than a tourist of life. Sontag was equally hard on herself, pointing out that she had become complacent in the face of her adoring husband. As in her essays, which call for a fresh response to art, she called herself to attention, saying she wanted to "re-open my nerves" (202). She had to awaken herself from the self-enclosed dullness of a marriage that prevented her from engaging with others.

Part of Sontag's reinvention of herself occurred when she moved from Paris to New York in early 1959. Although the city's griminess appalled her, she also threw herself into this new scene with gusto, paraphrasing the poet William Blake: "Exuberance is beauty" (210). On a daily level, she was ground down by her scut work at *Commentary* magazine and by her inability to openly admit her homosexuality (the term she used). Her guilt over her sexuality inhibited her and made her feel vulnerable. This major theme in her life, the dread of being exposed, is carefully hidden in her work, and yet it fueled so much of her writing about topics like camp.

Although Sontag had forsaken an academic career, the prospect of teaching the history of religion at Columbia University in 1960 was preferable to her unsatisfying work at *Commentary*. She enjoyed lecturing about Kant, who spoke to her own sense of tension between "inclination + sense of duty," which she enjoyed discussing with her students in "marvellous classes" (224). She had similar positive experiences at City College, but then in the spring semester at Sarah Lawrence College, where she was teaching philosophy, she began to show up late and unprepared for class, noting on February 29, 1960, that she could not seem to find a balance between "total enslavement to a responsibility and ostrich-like irresponsibility" (253), which again posed for her a Kantian dilemma.

Amid doubts about her own sensuality that broke through her intellectualizing, she again quoted Blake on life as "a little curtain of flesh on the bed of our desire" (228)—a phrase that brings to mind her call in *Against Interpretation* for an "erotics of art" to replace the "hermeneutics of art." Even as Sontag was making up and breaking up with her lover, the Cuban playwright Maria Irene Fornés, she was reading the novelist Stendhal and the philosopher Ortega y Gasset on the nature of love and also thinking about Emma Hamilton, who would become one of the main characters in *The Volcano Lover*. "What did this concealed woman have that these great men loved her" (238), Sontag wondered. These thoughts seem to arise out of her unsatisfying lovemaking with Fornés and Sontag's own doubts about what her actual feelings were. This uncertainty would suffuse her treatment of conflicted erotic affairs in *The Benefactor* and *Death Kit*.

It is no wonder that Emma Hamilton, a woman who gave so much of herself to her lovers, should fascinate Sontag, who bewailed her fear of loving Harriet and of defying Philip. Her marriage, she implied, was the only way to deal with her two lovers. Neither relationship sufficed, however, and Sontag did not see herself "as free" (299). She took up almost as a chant the phrase "Do something" (314), which she repeated three times. She seems paralyzed in this early 1960s period as she created a character, Hippolyte, who "serenely claims to be responsible for his acts, but patently is more haunted than he admits" (315). The same could be said of Sontag, who appeared, in public, so sovereign and self-contained and yet in her diaries confessed to a fundamental indecisiveness.

In the second volume of Sontag's diaries, *As Consciousness is Harnessed to Flesh: Journals and Notebooks 1964–1980*, nothing changes—insofar as she remained, in David Rieff's characterization, a perpetual student, forever reflecting on her education and making lists of words, books, and movies. However, the haughty Susan Sontag, so often written about in the memoirs of her friends, emerges. As Rieff also notes, his mother's definition of fool was, "to say the least, ecumenical" (10). She became the teacher as much as the student, an extravagant admirer of great writers but also a diva insisting on her own prerogatives. Rieff does not say so, but part of Sontag's assumption of arrogance grew out of her injunctions to herself in earlier diaries: she admired stars like Bette Davis, Joan Crawford, and Ida Lupino—all ladies, she noted, with cruel tongues who used men badly. This was the mark of the high-class femme fatale, always a little aloof with her admirers. "Didn't I despise Jacob [Taubes] for trying to be charming" (245), she noted in a diary entry in early 1960. And like a femme fatale in a forced confession, she wrote, "I have always betrayed people to each other" (242)—in this case because of her wanton gossiping about the sex lives of others. And perhaps most revealing of all is how she hardened herself with injunctions such as this: "Don't be kind. Kindness is not a virtue. Bad for people you're kind to. It's to treat them as inferiors, etc." (232) This disciplined ruthlessness became a defining feature, a measure of her own importance.

Of Sontag's politics, Rieff, in some embarrassment, excuses his mother's more fanciful comments about North Vietnam by emphasizing how appalled she was at the horrors of war. Russian dissident and exile Joseph Brodsky helped set Sontag straight on the subject of Communism, Soviet and otherwise, Rieff reports, as well as becoming her touchstone for how a great writer should think and behave. If Brodsky deepened her understanding of politics, he also encouraged her arrogance. They exercised their sense of superiority by belittling others.

And yet the opening diary entries for 1964 place Sontag in the same abject position she occupied when in love with Harriet Sohmers. This time the beloved was Maria Irene Fornés, whose very identity, Sontag declared, was predicated on her rejection of Sontag, who became the scapegoat for Fornés's every disappointment. Fornés could absolve herself by attacking Sontag. And it was just as vital, Sontag insisted, for her to cling to Fornés. Why? Sontag never quite said. But it seems that both in her love life and in her literary affairs she felt the need of a figure whom she could portray as lording it over her. Certainly in *Under the Sign of Saturn,* Sontag performed a kind of obeisance to the difficult writers she considered her superiors.

David Rieff suggests that the diaries constitute a kind of novel around which Sontag shaped her life, turning what was almost surely a different story from Fornés's point of view into a kind of master/slave scenario that attracted Sontag when she wrote about the pornography of the Marquis de Sade or in her own creation of Hippolyte, who sells his mistress, Frau Anders, into slavery. Only fragments of Fornés's point of view figure in Sontag's diary—for example, when Sontag reported on May 5, 1964, Fornés's claims that Sontag had damaged Fornés's ego (2). Who, then, was the master, who the slave? "Conceiving all relationships as between a master and a slave" (45), Sontag wrote in an entry for November 17, 1964, still insisting that it had been her role to play the slave in most relationships.

In 1964 Sontag made quite a study of Marlene Dietrich in the films of Josef von Sternberg. She liked the way the director "mounted" (26) the actress, making her a kind of complete object, a showpiece, much as the artist Joseph Cornell would later put Sontag in one of his famous boxes, emphasizing her as a diva. The high gloss of Dietrich's films fascinated Sontag, who was preoccupied with style, with the manner of presentation that becomes, as well, the artist's substance. The exotic nature of Dietrich's performances appealed to a writer who noted her "ostentatious appetite" (27) and proclivity for unusual food, which she consumed with the same voracity she demonstrated for so many different kinds of art in *Against Interpretation*. It is no wonder, then, that she began to make notes about camp, which above all attends to style, to the mode of presentation. She was reading, as well, the French new novelists, and listening to avant-garde music—all of which dislocated traditional realism, harmony, plot, and character development.

Sontag rarely commented on the quality of what she was reading. As in *Against Interpretation,* her choices may have in themselves conferred a certain distinction on the works she discussed, but if they were worthy, she felt no need to criticize. Criticism, she stated quite emphatically in her diary, was for inferior work, which she rarely deigned to examine. She focused rather on painters, sculptors, filmmakers, and writers who advanced their work by saturating themselves in the history of their art. The camp sensibility, for example, is all about those who are aware of how works of art contribute to or upend the history out of which they arise. Sontag saw herself as a vehicle for that history more than as an artist engaging in self-expression. Camp, with its focus on style, charted the changes in art, and camp's consciousness of style amounted to an understanding of the historicity of art. She wanted to see the artist's life only in terms of his art and collected quotations that said as much—such as Austrian composer Anton von Webern's assertion that "every life is a defense of a particular form" (54).

In 1965, while preparing to write her second novel, *Death Kit,* Sontag noted that William Burroughs in *Naked Lunch* switched from first- to third-person narration abruptly while also displaying his erudition in parentheses—techniques she also put to use in Diddy's wavering consciousness of his own imminent death. Life. as she noted in a diary entry for November 1, 1964, is the world; death is what is inside the head (43).

During this mid-1960s period, Sontag continued to look for models to emulate—writers whose styles she admired, artists who had certain manners that appealed to her. The painter Jasper Johns, for example, became not only a romantic attachment but also the epitome of the person and the artist she wanted to become. She admired his disputatious disposition and emulated it in essays that invited counterarguments. Yet she also observed a "formidable reticence" (59) that seems to have influenced her writing about the silences in works by Beckett and others. In actor Joseph Chaikin she found another version of holding back, a restraint, Chaikin told her, that stimulated "something in himself to come out" (71).

Sontag considered several different novel plots, listing them without comment. A few center on the intense relationship between two women (one variation is about two incestuous sisters), a theme, of course, in her own life but also in her study of Bergman's *Persona*. She contemplated re-creating characters such as Orpheus and Eurydice in dialogue but also science fiction plots and murder stories involving matricide and assassination. Other story ideas deal with a work of art, a discovered lost manuscript. She made one cryptic reference to a story based on Simone Weil's religious experience and Sylvia Plath's honest depiction of sex. The listing of so many narrative possibilities and allusions to Homer, Virgil, Herman Hesse, and Georges Bataille reveal an encyclopedic sensibility that suffuses so much of her nonfiction prose. The role of science fiction and fantasy predominated in these musings, which would eventually inform several of the stories in *I, etcetera,* a collection that plays with notions of identities. One day, Sontag supposed, the self could be rewired and reprogrammed.

Even as Sontag admired avant-garde artists such as Alain Robbe-Grillet and Antonin Artaud, she continued to muse over her attraction to *An American Tragedy* (1925), Theodore Dreiser's naturalistic novel that would seem the antithesis of the experimental, innovative fiction that she wished to write.[3] Describing what was "good" about the novel, she noted how intelligently Dreiser treated his main character, Clyde Griffiths, who murders his lover. She also praised the novelist's patient piling up of detail, reworked imaginatively in a way that also reflected the writer's Tolstoy-like compassion. This devotion to Dreiser seems to have inspired her own desire to create a story about a murder of some kind, which she did in *Death Kit,* although she did not emulate Dreiser's documentary focus—instead opting for a phantasmagorical, Poe-like narrative that allowed her to probe the subject of madness, a subject that often recurs in her mid-1960s diaries and that had already been explored in *The Benefactor.*

By the summer of 1965, Sontag had become acutely conscious of her public persona and of how she wanted to present herself. She decided to give no more interviews, she declared to her diary, until she could speak as forthrightly as Lillian Hellman did in her *Paris Review* interview. Indeed, Sontag did not sanction her own *Paris Review* interview until shortly before publication of her fourth novel, *In America,* since she regarded this particular publication as establishing the interview of record, the one that would be read as the author's definitive statement.

Above all, Sontag wanted the work of art to reign supreme, to change people's thinking, to be a solid object that would be as integrated as "consciousness is harnessed to flesh" (84), she wrote on May 22, 1965. She tried to embody this idea of the artwork in June 8, 1965, in notes about a novel concentrating on Thomas Faulk, a painter. Like Jasper Johns, Faulk is taciturn and short-tempered. He suffers the torments of a hypochondriac and takes injections for an unspecified malady. Like her earlier male protagonists, he seems to be going through a breakdown, although in another version she reversed herself, calling Faulk a "spiritual aristocrat," who would have no breakdowns.

Sontag seems to have been, by her own account, in a state of creative paralysis because she could not work out any sort of balanced life with Fornés. Sontag's moods fluctuated between longing and anger. Her son, David, served as her ballast, preventing her from giving way to suicidal thoughts. She explored her sadomasochistic tendencies with a New York City therapist, Diana Kemeny. Sontag's friend, the film critic Noël Burch, pointed out her contempt for others' weaknesses even as Sontag herself worried about her deference to anyone who seemed an authority. And yet, as she reported in a diary entry for August 28, 1965 (104), she had her own train of men she led on, including Burch and George Lichtheim (a Marxist historian).

Looking for new sources of inspiration, and perhaps experiences that would relieve her anxiety, she traveled to visit the writer Paul Bowles in Tangier, where Alfred Chester—at one time her close friend—was also visiting. The manic Chester, for all his delusions, had created the kind of fiction Sontag wished to emulate. She even took the title of a Chester novel, *I, Etc.,* and appropriated it for her own purposes. She noted that he did not try to establish time sequences and did not rely on a main character but instead assembled an enviable array of personalities. She would do the same in her short story collection, *I, etcetera.*

Sontag does not seem to have seen the irony of her irritated dismissal of Chester, who had become quite paranoid. She accused him of always seeking an "oracle" (105), a quest that she had also undertaken, including the days she spent with Chester in Paris, when she was first breaking away from her marriage and attempting to establish herself as a writer. And she described herself as falling for bullies like Harriet, Irene, and Alfred—all of whom became, for a time, her masters. The very idea of mastery, of being a master, is one aspect of her work in *Under the Sign of Saturn*. But Sontag's stay in Morocco was troubled because she could not accept what she called the "international homosexual style" (108), as exemplified by her host, Paul Bowles, and his wife, Jane. To Sontag it was a cruel, heartless, and obsessive circle, and also one without much sense of mission. In this drug-taking environment in which kif "melts the brain" (109), she would not be able to write. She compared the stupor and disorientation of these writers in Tangier to de Sade's insane asylum in Paris. She did not explain why she had been drawn to this alien group, except that it reminded her of that first weekend with her first lover, Harriet, when as a college student at Berkeley she was introduced to the gay and lesbian bar scene in San Francisco.

The figure of the artist, Thomas Faulk, continued to concern Sontag, but the nature of his project, the art he was supposed to create, is never quite revealed in the diaries, and perhaps that is one reason why Sontag abandoned the novel. So much of what she wrote about Faulk is cryptic because his background and attitudes are never clarified in the same way in which Sontag explored the art of her actress, Maryna Zaleska, in *In America*. Faulk seemed, in other words, too much of an abstraction of the artist, and he lacked the substantiality of Sontag's attachment to writers like Borges, who established the labyrinthine and ambiguous nature of human relations and the art that fails to resolve the world's paradoxes but heightens an awareness of the gap between life and art, which was, in Sontag's view, the artist's true subject.

The indeterminate nature of art was a key concept for Sontag, who rejected the notion of art as self-expression, as the record of insights she attributed to herself. Her thought, she insisted in a diary entry for November 20, 1965, did not drive her writing—not even in her diaries. On the contrary, the writing generated the thought. The writing of one day might very well yield different thoughts from the day before (143). The person Susan Sontag was a "banality" (149), she claimed a week later, when considering what she had said to her psychiatrist. The person does not count, only the professional. She liked to remain undecided about ideas, keeping them open, as Jasper Johns did.

Sontag saw herself as in the service of ideas. Although her diary entry for January 4, 1966, acknowledges the high quality of her mind, she did not rank herself as a genius—not on the level of Schopenhauer, Nietzsche, Wittgenstein, or Sartre. The greatest thinkers had been demonic, she argued, and she was just too conventional in comparison to them and not "mad enough" (168).

Sontag paralleled her search for master thinkers with a restless travel itinerary, which she documented, David Rieff reports, at the beginning of a notebook dated 1966–67. From June 3 to September 21, 1966, she journeyed to London, Paris, Prague, Venice, Antibes, and back and forth between these locations. Sometimes she took her son, David, along with her. He was both a comfort and a distraction. With him, she still felt lonely; with him, she also felt like another person. She could not be herself. So much of the diary, in fact, is about Sontag's frustration with not being herself, or with not measuring up to the self she thought she could become. She wanted to convert her experience—her travels and her reading—into a novel that kept changing in form. Should it be epistolary, a diary, an annotated poem, an encyclopedia, a confession, a list, a manual, or a compendium of documents? All of these already constituted the very diary in which she was jotting down these possibilities.

Sontag thought about how the world turns itself into an aesthetic experience. She visited the catacombs in Paris, and it was there that she explored a tunnel that later became the tunnel of death in *Death Kit,* although her diary does not make the connection. It is characteristic of her to dwell on the artistic treatment of death by referring in the same sentence to horror films and to Mario Praz's famous work of scholarship *Romantic Agony,* and also to reading Foucault on the subject of madness, which, in Foucault's words, is the "absolute break with the work of art" (171). In Sontag's first two novels, the self disintegrates as Hippolyte and Diddy dissolve into their stories, unable to accomplish the feat of individuality that marks the bildungsroman.

The artist-thinker who self-destructs was very much a part of Sontag's thinking and her experience. Her best friend, Susan Taubes, committed suicide and became the subject of a Sontag story, "Debriefing," and in Sontag's diary entry for June 26, 1966, she noted without comment, in lines set out like a poem:

> Sylvia Plath:
> Poet—
> Husband, father
> Two children—
> Suicide— (174)

Sontag experienced both the euphoria and the ennui of marriage, the struggle to establish herself as a writer, the haunting yearning for a father who had died when she was quite young, her own role as mother—all of which bound her to Plath, although suicide never seems to have had any appeal to Sontag except as the absolute way of defining a response to life. Sontag was, however, subject to depression and understood the state of mind that led to madness or suicide. On July 5, 1966, Sontag placed her fictional character, Thomas Faulk, just above the name "Sylvia Plath" (176) in quotation marks, as though Plath had become, like Faulk, a character in Sontag's mind, Sontag's language. The use of quotation marks is noteworthy because of the way Sontag employed them in *Against Interpretation,* where "Adolf Hitler," for example, was treated as both a historical figure but also as Leni Riefenstahl's invention. In other words, there was a real Adolf Hitler but also "Adolf Hitler." Incipient, then, in Sontag's thinking, was a way to take on history and yet still represent it as a fiction, a mode of imagination she would practice in both *The Volcano Lover* and *In America.*

Sontag's diaries, full of cryptic jottings, lists, and random thoughts, seem like so many dead ends, fragments of selves and stories that never quite congeal. As with the poem-like evocation of Plath, the diary passages seem opaque plaques of thought that Sontag could not quite figure out. These passages also seem, given the peripatetic nature of her existence, thoughts caught on the fly, picked up and put down at a moment's notice, reflecting the intermittent nature of Sontag's cerebration.

In an entry composed on June 26, 1966, in Paris, Sontag considered a novel that would have a narrator questioning who he is, where he is, and to whom he is talking, while also wondering what would happen next. Would this be a work of science fiction? Sontag's diary is not clear on this point, but her desire to create a work not limited by the conventions of realism, or by the ordinary limits of language, seems evident in her quotations from Wittgenstein: "The limits of my language are the limits of my world" and "To imagine a language means to imagine a life" (174). Rather than seeing fiction as a representation of a world already formed, she struggled to conceive of a novel that is itself the world as created by her narrator. But she had already attempted precisely such a novel in *The Benefactor* and *Death Kit,* and it would be decades before she would relinquish Wittgenstein in favor of the most traditional form of all: the historical novel, which she would try to revive by insisting that fiction could rewrite history.

Sontag's diaries reveal her uncertainty about the medium she wanted to explore. Writing in Paris on July 28, 1966, she observed that documentary film (she would eventually make one, *Promised Lands*) had a special authority, like the photograph, because it seemed to be an "image of reality." Theater, on the other hand, was a "representation rather than a presentation" (182). So how could theater seem as authentic as documentary film? And yet plays like *The Brig* and *Marat/Sade* (the subject of an essay in *Against Interpretation*) had a vitality and vision that superseded most documentaries, or so it seems since Sontag singled them out while mentioning no specific documentary film. Television, she recognized, was becoming all encompassing, making Vietnam the "first television war" (182). She contrasted Artaud's idea of a theater that transforms consciousness with television's overwhelming presentation of images that dilute awareness. The ability of images to attenuate thought, if not obliterate it, would become one of the main contentions of *On Photography*.

Television's tendency to display undifferentiated images is treated as almost a personal affront in Sontag's diaries. She quoted her friend the actor Joseph Chaikin as saying, "I look to be offended" (184). Any medium that did not discriminate, carefully select, and distinguish troubled her, although in later years, especially in *Regarding the Pain of Others*, she expressed doubt that the plethora of images seen in photographs and on television do necessarily dull the senses and judgment. She recognized, in other words, that her arguments were exaggerations, unproven and open to correction.

In this period (August 1966), Sontag settled in London to watch the Polish director Jerzy Grotowski and British director Peter Brook rehearse their actors. Grotowski seemed to be putting on the stage a drama of human behavior that she treated with irony in *The Benefactor*. Exactly what Sontag meant is not clear, but it seems she was attracted to Grotowski's experimental handling of actors who take possession of the stage, eschewing props, and making the performing space a projection of their characters' thoughts and feelings, much as the narrative space in Sontag's first two novels is a world emanating from her narrators, not a world her narrators simply inhabit or respond to. Grotowski fascinated her because, while Sontag treated her ideas as literary conceits, he took his own ideas as literally true. Thus she described Ryszard Cieslak, Grotowski's celebrated star, as appearing virtually without clothes on a platform with the other characters revolving around him emitting a fantastic energy. The centripetal effect of this theater movement is what seems to have aroused Sontag, perhaps because it was a concrete manifestation, an embodiment of her early fiction.

Peter Brook had to translate everything Grotowski said, so that, in Sontag's words, it was like watching a French movie with subtitles. Everything the British actors learned about the Grotowski method was filtered through Brook's voice and manner, which, she noted, only increased Brook's authority. The Brook and Grotowski dynamic resembled the doubling of authority figures in Sontag's two Swedish films, which present two sensibilities reflecting Sontag's bifurcated biography straddled between the worlds of London and Paris, and Paris and New York.

Although Sontag had given up the idea of an academic career, her diary reveals that well into the 1960s she still contemplated completing her Ph.D. with a thesis about consciousness of self in contemporary French philosophy. Her reading of Sartre, Georges Bataille, and Maurice Blanchot, coupled with her observations of Grotowski, whose seeming inertness fascinated her (as though he exemplified the aesthetics of silence), perhaps suggested the possibility of writing an academic work. She made a list exploring the roles of language, silence, art, religion, and Eros in the development and manipulation of self-consciousness. Interspersed with such ideas is, again, the figure of Grotowski himself, a kind of black column, dressed in shiny black shoes, black socks, and sunglasses. He seems almost to be a character in a fiction taking shape in Sontag's diary and conceivably part of the two novellas she projected, both of which would have a theatrical presentation.

Role-playing in the theater, by its very nature, appealed to Sontag's notion of the self as a creation of consciousness. But in her diary her various roles seem discontinuous: woman, mother, lover, teacher. How did they consort with one another? Part of Sontag's confusion seems to have derived from her fraught relationship with her mother, which the diary treats at great length, showing how as a very young child Sontag's mother demanded so much emotional support from her daughter that the daughter felt superior to the mother and craved her mother's dependence so that Sontag could "become strong" and "stronger than 'the others'" (211). This dynamic of dependence led to what Sontag called her cannibalizing of others' experiences for her own purposes and the search for a project worthy of her ambitions and her "cosmic, voyaging mind" (213), as she put it in the long diary entry for August 9, 1967. That mind set her apart from her surroundings as definitively as Hippolyte's dreaming does in *The Benefactor*. What made the affair with Fornés so disturbing is that Fornés forced Sontag to look at herself—that is, to use her mind for more than observing the world outside herself. The failure of Sontag's first two protagonists, Hippolyte and Diddy, to break out of their solipsism is a fate Sontag barely escaped herself, and with Fornés's help, even though that help caused Sontag great pain. Sontag had scaled down herself to fit at least somewhat comfortably in the lives of her family and friends, but Fornés showed the tremendous cost to Sontag of creating an unexamined self. In a striking phrase, Sontag referred to the "desexualized pedagogic friendship" (213) she specialized in before the advent of Fornés. The safety of dispassionate relationships meant that Sontag had failed to develop a complete self. It is no wonder, then, that even an academic study of self-consciousness would have considerable appeal to her. Only recently and fitfully had she been able to break her usual cycle of building up a new friend and then seeing that friend's flaws, followed by the evasive approach-avoidance brand of intimacy and withdrawal that is so characteristic of her characters in *Duet for Cannibals*, *Brother Carl*, and *Unguided Tour*.

Theater and film became so much a part of Sontag's psyche that she referred to the film stills on her walls as her "friends" (216), showing her a more glamorous world to which she aspired. Sontag noted her obsession with lists, suggesting that they are her way of establishing value—but in a self-contained world, since none of these pictures or characters could speak to her. The lists and posters were her way of maintaining her world (217), much as the constant allusions to artists and works of art bind together books like *Against Interpretation*.

In several diary entries in late 1967, Sontag accused herself of bad faith, of not really giving herself to Fornés as Sontag had promised to do. These passages shift away from a concern with the aesthetic view of life (as represented in *The Benefactor*) to the ethical view of *Death Kit,* as Sontag herself noted. Diddy is, in effect, forced to acknowledge the world outside himself—or at the very least to question the world inside himself—as Sontag repeatedly did with herself in her diaries. But how to move beyond the aesthetic/ethical dualism continued to perplex her.

Sontag's involvement in political causes, especially in protests against the Vietnam War, seemed to contribute to her retreat from novel writing. Although she continued to write short, experimental pieces of fiction, she devoted most of her writing not only to nonfiction but to political commentary. Her diaries, according to David Rieff, include reports on her trip to Hanoi that he chose not to publish because they contained factual reports and "historical notations" (237) as well as lists of Vietnamese words. Except for a few representative examples of this reportorial material, he includes only one analytical entry about her trip, which, he implies, is more critical than what she published in *Trip to Hanoi.*

In an undated entry (Rieff estimates it was written on May 5 or 6, 1968, in Hanoi), Sontag expressed her frustration with the language barrier that made it hard not to speak in the simplest phrases through a translator. She felt infantilized, bundled along like a child in a carefully selected tour of certain sites. Even worse, she found herself behaving like an A student, eager to perform well for her hosts. She noted their rigid, formulaic hospitality, and at the start it looked as though learning anything of consequence was hopeless. The Vietnamese seemed to have no idea of how to treat her, or how she might react to their treatment of her. Yet she knew it was not what she had come to learn that was important but rather that her trip was a "piece of political theatre" (239). This aspect of her trip is never mentioned in *Trip to Hanoi,* which is perhaps one reason why David Rieff finds her published comments on North Vietnam so embarrassing. She never quite reckoned, in print, with the political ramifications of her trip. She was simply following the Vietnamese script, she noted in her diary, and yet she was untroubled by this and even said that this is how it "should be." As she explained, she was part of a "corporate identity": "friends of the Vietnamese struggle" (239). And so the trip was the group's reward, their treat for their support and encouragement for the North Vietnamese cause. It was the propaganda value of the visit that counted, she realized. So the group was not required to do anything specific in terms of supporting the North or asking questions during this trip.

Sontag bridled at hearing the constant refrain that the North Vietnamese understood that the American people were their friends. They North Vietnamese knew nothing about America if they believed what they said, she noted, although what she thought of America is not stated. Her published work reflects considerable disdain for Americans and American history. The Vietnamese she met seemed without psychological complexity—a point that *is* made in *Trip to Hanoi,* which explores her uncomfortable realization that North Vietnamese culture had no place for someone like her, who thought like her, who questioned her own motivations. The Vietnamese were puzzled by her questions because they did not share her cross-cultural sensibility. As in *Trip to Hanoi,* she extolled the Cuban Revolution, finding in it a sensibility closer to her own and more relevant to the concerns of a sophisticated American like herself. North Vietnam was not a society where she felt free to talk about herself, to deal with personal concerns; instead, everyone seemed blanketed with a discreet and bland courteousness.

Especially distressing is Sontag's discovery—one that is not explored in *Trip to Hanoi*—that North Vietnam was a hierarchical society in which everyone knew their place. She much preferred the "populist manners" (242) of the Cuban revolution. She learned that government people got special privileges, and she was dismayed at how everyone seemed to think that to have this kind of elite was proper in a Communist country. She quoted a fellow writer, Andrew Kopkind, as wondering if the North Vietnamese had egos.

David Rieff includes some of Andrew Kopkind's comments about Sontag's activities in North Vietnam, presumably because Sontag herself did not write about how she described American culture to the Vietnamese. She evidently spoke at some length. Kopkind did report on Sontag's attacking Mark Sommer, an American journalist who praised the North Vietnamese for holding on to their humanity during the American bombing of their country. Sontag and Kopkind found Sommer's comments condescending. Kopkind also mentioned that Sontag went to visit American prisoners of war, but how she felt about them is not disclosed, and it is a subject not dealt with in *Trip to Hanoi.* Kopkind only remarked that Sontag gave the prisoners news about political changes in the United States.

By August 1968 Sontag was in Stockholm at work on the first of her two films made in Sweden. Her diary entry on August 7 is a long reflection on her emerging femininity, her discovery that she liked bright, colorful clothes and flowers, and this reveling in beautiful objects was such a change from the black, grey, and brown world of her marriage. The sources of her interest in camp and the emerging aesthetic that informs *Against Interpretation* are evident in passages about her involvement with the male homosexual world that had liberated her and made it more possible for her to be "more genuinely a woman" (254). These exuberant thoughts seemed to prepare for her expressed hope that one day someone who loved her would read her diaries and feel closer to her. In one of the few passages that deals directly with the purpose of the diaries, Sontag stated that the writing is for herself and that she felt edified by simply writing down her thoughts.

Curiously, Sontag's notebooks say nothing at all about filming in Sweden but are rather a record of her reading Chekhov, Melville, Tolstoy, Nabokov, Conrad, Agatha Christie, Artaud, and Adorno, as well as of her reflections on revolutionaries such as Lenin and Rosa Luxembourg—in response, perhaps, to the student revolt in France in 1968. From 1968 to 1970 she wrote very little in her diaries as she moved between Paris and New York, involved with a new lover, the Italian aristocrat Carlotta del Pezzo, a recovering drug addict whom Sontag had to treat warily because of Carlotta's fear that she would become dependent on Sontag. As in Sontag's first two novels, love was bound up with power, with concerns about who was the dominant figure in an affair. Sontag told herself that she needed to be strong but also permissive, an object of desire but not one that overwhelmed the beloved—a dynamic she explored in her essay "The Pornographic Imagination," included in *Styles of Radical Will*.

Women's issues and women's liberation began to filter into the diaries in the early 1970s, although Sontag's engagement with feminism as a political movement is fitful and quickly subsumed into her worries over her affair with Carlotta del Pezzo, an increasingly problematic relationship, according to Sontag, because Carlotta could not see herself as the author of her own existence. But the main problem, Sontag noted, is that she saw life as a series of "projects." Indeed, this is the key to her attitude toward herself and her writing: Both were in progress, which meant that Sontag felt incomplete, dissatisfied, and anxious about the outcome of her activities. In a long passage dated February 17, 1970, Sontag explored the nature of women in a way absent in her other writing. In her published work, her comments on feminism and Women's Liberation are usually expressions of solidarity, whereas in her diary she dwelt more on how women have represented the "Southern" (279) values of softness, amiability, and a mentality less concerned with ideas and more spontaneous and emotional than men. The exercise of the will is regarded as a masculine attribute, she suggested, and that made it difficult for Carlotta to assert herself.

Sontag's comments on her filmmaking began to inform the diaries in mid-1970. On July 16. 1970, for example, she noted that *Brother Carl* dealt with the nature of love, sadism, and masochism—all of which had pervaded her diary accounts of her love affairs with Harriet Sohmers, Maria Irene Fornés, and Carlotta del Pezzo. In fact, her writing the script for *Brother Carl* occurred as Sontag began to mourn the end of her affair with Carlotta. The movie, like the earlier *Duet for Cannibals*, is in part about love that is lost and cannot be repaired.

The early 1970s are an interregnum for Sontag, who had trouble writing an essay on women's liberation while working out why her love affairs had failed, mulling over an invitation to visit China, and the story that would become "Project for a Trip to China." Notes for essays on travel, death, revolution, film, and false starts on novels and films are strewn across entries for several days in the early 1970s. As David Rieff reports, Sontag's trip to China yielded very little material—only desultory notes in her diaries. Reflecting on both civil rights and women's liberation, Sontag declared herself a "pure integrationist" in a January 7, 1973, entry, affirming her opposition to "sex-specific standards" (353). The stories she found she could write, like "Debriefing" and "Baby," were autobiographical. And she attributed this new vein in her work to her essay on Paul Goodman, which put her in touch with her American voice.

One of the most revealing diary entries was written on December 23, 1973, probing her bifurcated sensibility—part Flaubert, part Simone Weil, Sontag noted. Of the former she identified with his ambition, egotism, arrogance, sensuality, and dishonesty; and of the latter she cited ambition and egotism as well, but also an asceticism and quest for purity and honesty. These contradictions, Sontag believed, are at the heart of her paradoxical behavior. She was reading a biography of Weil and was dismayed at what she learned about the writer, especially Weil's denial of her sexuality and femininity, but Sontag's own puritanism (a term she often used in the diary in relation to herself) matched Weil's own desire for a life unencumbered by the body, an immaculate state that both Weil and Sontag associated with wisdom. This fascinating passage seems to explain why Sontag was so chary of dealing with herself in her nonfiction work—why, when she wrote about camp and AIDS, for example, she made no references to her own homosexuality.

By the mid-1970s Sontag was rethinking positions taken in *Against Interpretation*. She was looking for a new vocabulary. The culture had changed, and perhaps she had to engage in an argument with herself to refresh her views. No longer did it seem necessary to speak of liberation, especially since what seemed groundbreaking in the 1960s had since been absorbed into the mainstream. The New Left, she concluded, had not really created an alternative culture, and this recognition signals her reevaluation of the left, which seemed to be fighting old battles. Her entry for May 16, 1975, marks the beginning of an evolution in her politics that would become evident in her Town Hall speech calling Communism "Fascism with a human face."

Surrounded by a faithful, select circle of friends, and comforted by her new liaison with the French actress and producer Nicole Stéphane, Sontag reflected on her attraction to "custodial relationships" (384). In this case, Stéphane became the one to take care of Sontag as Sontag believed she had taken care of her mother, who made Sontag almost into a sibling and confidant. Out of the renewal of her life in Paris and New York and a continuing interest in film, Sontag found a way to refashion the ideas of *Against Interpretation* by attacking Leni Riefenstahl, whose work she had defended as art, even if its propaganda was fascist. On July 19, 1975, she came to the conclusion that there "really is a 'fascist aesthetics'" (388). It was not possible to speak simply of the form of Riefenstahl's *Triumph of the Will*. The politics governed or at least coexisted with the film's form. This entry asks over and over again what it means to employ aesthetic judgment alone without some kind of moral standard.

Sontag's diary is curiously silent about the breast cancer diagnosis that gave her very little chance of surviving the disease. The truncated nature of her entries is perhaps an indication of her exhaustion in the summer of 1976 during a period of intensive chemotherapy. She mentioned her fear once. Although in earlier entries she referred to her constant thoughts about death, such thoughts do not make an appearance as a response to her surgery and other medical treatments. One of the few comments on cancer comes from an intern at Sloan-Kettering who noted that the disease "doesn't knock at your door first." It is, Sontag added, "insidious," a "secret invasion" (408).

Even as she was recovering from cancer treatment, Sontag was reading Walter Benjamin and formulating the arguments about photography that would be yet another way for her to revisit the form/content nexus of *Against Interpretation* and *Styles of Radical Will*. And she was thinking of titles for what would ultimately become *Illness as Metaphor*. As Nicole Stéphane gradually faded from Sontag's life, the Russian writer and emigrant to America Joseph Brodsky took her place. He becomes in the diaries a kind of touchstone for Sontag's own opinions and observations. They argued as well, but Brodsky appears in the diaries almost as Sontag's other voice.

Sontag's growing interest in dance—she seems to have considered it superior to other arts in America—appears in her entry for February 25, 1979. Twyla Tharp's choreography, Sontag asserted, reconciled her to "being an American" (481). Full of ideas for stories and also a book she was planning to write about her visits to Japan, Sontag was seemingly energized by the imminent publication of her stories in *I, etcetera*. The death of Roland Barthes, which she announced in her diary on March 26, 1980, was a momentous event for her, since he was as important as Brodsky in sharing a kind of fellowship of ideas, but she seemed undisturbed and even measured about his passing, noting that while he became a "real writer," he could not "purge himself of his ideas" (503)—a statement that appears to reflect her own desire to abandon nonfiction prose for fiction. She was trying to make a transition that Barthes, by implication, was not able to achieve.

Although she was nearly a decade away from writing *The Volcano Lover,* her May 9, 1980, entry dwells on the pathos of the intellectual and the collector, two of the major themes of her novel. And here the diaries break off, to be resumed only when David Rieff publishes the third and final volume.

CHAPTER 9

The Legacy

In 1978 Sontag won the National Book Critics circle award for *On Photography*. In 1990 she won a MacArthur Fellowship. Italy awarded her the Malaparte Prize in 1992. In France she was the recipient of the Commandeur Ordre des Arts et des Lettres (1990). She won the National Book Award for her novel *In America* in 2000. She was awarded the Jerusalem Prize in 2001 and the George Polk Award in 2002, the former in recognition of her work on behalf of individual freedom and the latter for her brilliant article "Looking at War" in the *New Yorker*. In 2003, the year before she died, she was honored with the Prince Asturias Award for Literature and the Peace Prize of the German Book Trade. Her books have been translated into more than thirty languages. In 2014 the *New Republic* included Susan Sontag in its ranking of the most important thinkers of the last one hundred years.[1]

Perhaps more than any other American author, Sontag became a public figure, commenting on major political and cultural events, traveling to theaters of war in Vietnam and the former Yugoslavia, and serving as the model of an activist writer in the tradition of André Malraux and Ernest Hemingway. In famous essays such as "Notes on 'Camp'" and "Against Interpretation," she sought to explore and define the changing nature of popular and elite culture while producing her own experimental stories and novels. Although she modified many of her positions and even recanted some of her opinions, she remained a cynosure of the American critical establishment. And even after her death, she remains a touchstone for many cultural commentators.

Almost every year since her death in 2004, a new book by or about Susan Sontag has appeared: *Female Icons: Marilyn Monroe to Susan Sontag* by Carl Rollyson (2005); *Sontag and Kael: Opposites Attract Me* by Craig Seligman (2005); *At the Same Time: Essays and Speeches* (2007); *Reborn: Journals and*

Notebooks 1947–1963 (2008); *Swimming in a Sea of Death: A Son's Memoir* by David Rieff (2008); *Notes on Sontag* by Philip Lopate (2009); *The Scandal of Susan Sontag*, a collection of essays (2009); *Sempre Susan: A Memoir of Susan Sontag* by Sigrid Nunez (2011); *As Consciousness Is Harnessed to Flesh: Journals and Notebooks 1964–1980* (2012); *Dreaming in French: The Paris Years of Jacqueline Bouvier Kennedy, Susan Sontag, and Angela Davis* by Alice Kaplan (2012); and *Susan Sontag: The Complete Rolling Stone Interview* by Jonathan Cott (2013).

This continuing concern with Sontag's achievement is remarkable, since there is often a fallow period when even the greatest writers suffer neglect in the years immediately following their deaths. Not so with Sontag because she remains eminently quotable, far reaching in her interests and travels, and determined not only to make a mark on her time but to maintain adamantly the primary role of literature and the arts in the postmodern world. Her books and essays are taught in a wide variety of courses and disciplines—not surprising since she wrote about so many subjects: politics, medicine, literature, film, photography, and various aspects of popular culture. Her work in drama as a director and playwright and in fiction (especially as a historical novelist) is not generally regarded as highly as her nonfiction, but all aspects of her career continue to be discussed and debated because of her prominent role as a public intellectual.

APPENDIX

The Uncollected Susan Sontag

Nonfiction

Although Susan Sontag collected a substantial body of her work in book-length publications, significant articles and essays published in newspapers, journals, and magazines are uncollected and reflect important aspects of her thinking and of her career as writer. Discussing these pieces in chronological order is another way of gauging the range and implications of her interests.

Sontag's review of H. J. Kaplan's novel, *The Plenipotentiaries* in *Chicago Review* (Winter 1950, 49–50) was her first professional publication. Set in Paris, the novel concerns the love and powerful struggle between a couple that is reminiscent of *Duet for Cannibals*. The expatriate flavor of this fiction would naturally appeal to a writer already versed in the journals of André Gide and more attuned to cultural events in Europe than in the United States, as her memoir "Pilgrimage" reveals.

In her first years as an independent writer living in New York City, Sontag published a review in the *Columbia Daily Spectator* (November 18, 1960, 3–4, 8) of Tom F. Driver's *The Sense of History in Greek and Shakespearean Drama*. In "The History of Drama," she revealed her strong interest in the history of religion. Drawn to Driver's exploration of the Biblical (linear) and the cyclical senses of time in Hegel, Marx, Tillich, Nietzsche, Spengler, and Eliade, she confirmed Driver's argument that these different senses of time were muddled in discussions of drama. She also took issue with Daniel Bell's influential book *The End of Ideology* (1960), which contended that ideologies had been exhausted and are irrelevant. She rejected Bell's views because they simply endorsed the status quo.

In "Demons and Dreams," a review of I. B. Singer's novel *The Slave* (*Partisan Review*, Summer 1962, 460–63), Sontag favored his "power of sensuous evocation"—so different from most contemporary novels that psychologize characters. She called his depiction of Polish Jewry "pre-modern." His characters, products of a traditional society with a powerful sense of community, seemed to her to point the way to a revival of fiction that could "renew our capacities for emotional catharsis." Sensuous, a key word in the Sontag lexicon, defined for her the art she extolled in *Against Interpretation*.

The Garden by Yves Berger is a first novel Sontag touted in "Virginia Is a State of Mind" (*New York Herald Tribune Book Week*, September 15, 1963, 18, 28) as an "interior meditation," the kind of *nouveau roman* she would endorse in *Against Interpretation*. She called the novel a philosophical romance—a term that could also apply to her first novel, *The Benefactor*. In fact, the novel is revealed as the book Berger has just written, just as Sontag's novel is an extension of Hippolyte's dreams.

"A Voluptuary's Catechism" (*New York Herald Tribune Book Week*, October 6, 1963, 6, 21) clearly foreshadows Sontag's later writing about pornography in *Styles of Radical Will*. In her review of Jean Genet's *Our Lady of the Flowers*, she insisted that his indulgence in cruelty and sexual perversity is not pornographic, but spiritual, because of his "shamelessly aesthetic" manner of presentation.

"A New Life for an Old One," a review of John Hawkes's novel *Second Skin* (*New York Times Book Review*, April 5, 1964, 5), staked out Sontag's quarrel with the contemporary American novel. Unlike Bernard Malamud's novel *A New Life*, which just reports the story of a man experiencing joy in a reborn life, Hawkes enacts this sense of renewal in a style that transcends the boundaries of Malamud's realism. If Hawkes's handling of certain details and emotions seems too understated, she contended, his work nevertheless is a considerable achievement. Sontag revealed a similar bias in "Laughter in the Dark," a review of James Purdy's novel *Cabot Wright Begins* in the *New York Times Book Review* (October 25, 1964, 5), preferring his antirealistic novel *Malcolm* to his current novel's snapshot picture of small-town American life.

In general, during this period, Sontag welcomed work that brought new energy not only to fiction but also to the theater. She reviewed *Inadmissible Evidence* by British playwright John Osborne, commenting in "Vogue's Notebook: Theatre" (*Vogue*, August 15, 1965, 51–52) that the London production brought "new energy" into the predictable well-made play patented in West End theaters. But in performance the play also seemed "shallow, exhibitionistic, fragmented."

In "Pop Goes the Easel" (*New York Herald Tribune Book Week*, July 25, 1965, 1, 12–13), Sontag reviewed two books (John Rublowsky's *Pop Art* and Henry Geldzahler's *American Painting in the Twentieth Century*), deploring their vapid styles and labeling of pop art, which misread artists like Jasper Johns and Andy Warhol, whose work have an ironic sensibility and consciousness of the history of art that these critics failed to acknowledge. In short, she was calling for a more sophisticated criticism. This piece probably was not included in *Against Interpretation* because its tone departs from her desire to endorse good work and promising critical approaches. Similarly, "Apocalypse in a Paint Box" (*Washington Post Book World*, November 21, 1965, 4, 26–27) faulted Maurice Nadeau's *The History of Surrealism* for not clearly assessing what no longer was important about the movement or what remained of it that was relevant. She argued that more attention should be directed to Surrealism's modernist thrust, concerned with "complexities and contradictions" that remain a challenge to traditional definitions of art. In this article, Sontag began to work out her extended argument about Surrealism that appears in *On Photography*.

At the earliest stages of her publishing career, Sontag took on reference book assignments. Thus in the "Literature" entry for *The Great Ideas of Today*, 1966 (146–91), she divided her discussion of the year into five categories: "Realism," "The Avant-Garde," "The Joycean Tradition," "The Literature of Extreme Situations, and "Literature: Between Art and Life." Her discussion of these categories was bound by three principles: By literature she meant works of art, works of thought, which, in turn, narrowed to art or literature that was "in a state of crisis." She discussed writers such as Graham Greene, Iris Murdoch, and Flannery O'Connor, who remained in the realist tradition, creating plots considered credible and complex characters who speak in an "ordinary" language easily assimilated by readers. Realism was still the dominating force in fiction, written as though such great experimentalists as James Joyce, Virginia Woolf, Samuel Beckett, and Gertrude Stein had never existed. A few contemporaries, such as William Burroughs and Laura Riding, wrote in a more analytical and intellectual mode, in styles she deemed cinematic, plotless, fragmented, and from shifting points of view. A writer such as William Gass, in *Omsetter's Luck*, continued the Joycean tradition of poetic prose filled with an exuberant, experimental energy. Writers as various as Foucault and Nabokov explored extreme states of consciousness, including madness, and employed an inventive language that implicitly undermined the realist tradition. Sontag concluded this survey with recommending Robbe-Grillet's playful, mind-altering prose, which elevated the creativity of art and liberated it from the realist tradition.

In "Transmitting His Master's Voice," a review of *A Psycho-Analytic Dialogue: The Letters of Sigmund Freud and Karl Abraham, 1907–1926* (*Washington Post Book World*, April 3, 1966, 2–3, 12–13), Sontag emphasized the two men's shared Jewishness and dedication to making a map out of psychoanalytic ideas presented in a clear, rational system. This is the scientific model, she pointed out, which Freud insisted on because his system could then be shared and replicated by others. The alternative, treating psychoanalysis as an art, necessarily places emphasis on the creator, on the individual and on art's quest not exclusively for knowledge but for pleasure. Pleasure, of course, is a key value that Sontag associated with Roland Barthes, who emphasized that art is a means of discovery but does not lead to some end outside of itself. In her preface to Barthes's *Writing Degree Zero* (1968), she contrasted Barthes's interest in literature as process with Sartre's notion of writing as product.

"Yugoslav Report: Writers and Conferences" (*Partisan Review,* Winter 1966, 116–23) reflects Sontag's early interest in PEN long before she became president of the American PEN Center. While expressing disappointment in the talks, which seemed to ignore the specific concerns of writers, and with the sparse attendance of important writers, she was impressed with the goodwill of those who considered themselves part of a worldwide literary community. For an American, Sontag noted, such conferences helped dispel provinciality. She was cool toward Arthur Miller's plan to increase the American role in the organization, thus signaling her already well-established preference for European modes of thoughts and for those European writers who exemplified her own dedication to literature.

Sontag's lack of interest in the contemporary American novel, evident in *Against Interpretation,* may explain why she did not include "The Avant-Garde and Contemporary Literature" (*Wilson Library Quarterly,* June 1966, 930–32, 937–40) in her collection of essays. Her definition of avant-garde went beyond the generally understood notion of a movement that challenges traditional art and creates new art form. The avant-garde has an epistemology, Sontag argued, which rejects the contemporary novel's slavish adherence to representation and imitation. The novel, Sontag suggested, can stand by itself and create its own meaning, rather then remain dependent on some construct of reality outside itself to which it must be faithful.

One of Sontag's earliest political pieces, "We Are Choking with Shame and Anger," published in *Teach-Ins: U.S.A.; Reports, Opinions, Documents,* 345–49), edited by Louis Menasche and Ronald Radosh and published by Praeger in 1967, is a speech originally delivered at Town Hall in Manhattan, urging Vietnam War protestors not to be consumed by their outrage, converting it only into rhetoric. Indignation, she cautioned, was not enough. On the contrary, she recommended self-questioning, a form of inquiry into one's own motivations that she would later conduct (fitfully) on herself in "Trip to Hanoi."

The more strident, programmatic side of Sontag's thinking is displayed in her untitled piece in ¡Viva Che! Contributions in Tribute to Ernesto 'Che' Guevara, edited by Marianne Alexandre (London: Lorrimer, 1968, 106–10). She extolled the Cuban revolutionary as the "most unequivocal image of the *humanity* of the world-wide revolutionary struggle." At this stage in her career,

Sontag still believed that contemporary Marxists, especially those in the post-colonial and developing countries, could develop a model of Communism that would redeem the "traumatic betrayal" by Stalinists. Guevara was important because of his commitment to the international cause of liberation, which, Sontag insisted, was founded on "*democratic* practices."

In part, Sontag looked to Guevara as a kind of redeemer because of her view of her own country as "a vast sickening menace to the peace of the world," as she put it in "Perspectives on the Coming Elections" in *Win* (March 31, 1968, 3–5). American society would change only over a long period if radicals continued to organize into effective groups and promoted a deepening consciousness of the radical changes required in American society. While the two-party system prevailed, and voting for one party or the other would make a concrete difference, radicals nevertheless had to work at enlarging the scope of debate.

"Some Thoughts on the Right Way (for Us) to Love the Cuban Revolution" appeared in *Ramparts* magazine (April 1969, 6, 10, 14, 16, 18–19)—then perhaps the most important widespread vehicle for radical thought and coverage of contemporary events. This article was also the culmination of Sontag's early period of radicalization, when nothing seemed more urgent than finding new models of revolutionary and democratic societies to serve in the protest against what Sontag saw as America's rapacious and corrupt capitalism with imperialistic designs on the rest of the world. But the New Left no longer viewed itself as merely opposing a political system in the same terms as the old left. The former was engaging in what Sontag called a "psychic revolution" that challenged "basic cultural norms." Members of the New Left focused on freedom of the self and were more provincial than their radical predecessors. This very individualism made the New Left misinterpret the Cuban revolution, which was not so much about the liberation of individuals as it was about empowering a whole society with a revolutionary consciousness. Unlike American radicals, Cuban revolutionaries had no Protestant ethic to rebel against, no tradition of concern with the reform of the soul and self, and as a result Cubans were more community minded then their radical American counterparts. Cubans therefore did not share the American radicals' rejection of American culture. A Cuban revolutionary's commitment to the public sphere, in other words, did not come with the kind of psychological baggage that informed American radicals rebelling against their upbringings. Cuban internationalism was more connected to what was happening in world capitals such as Rome or Stockholm than was the case with the New Left. Sontag saw a certain lack of discipline in American dissenters fixated on what was wrong with American culture. She urged the new generation of Americans to think more in terms of what was happening in other parts of the world and less on their quarrel with traditional

American values. In effect, she was suggesting that the Cuban Revolution had its own value that Americans needed to absorb, instead of projecting an American program on what was happening in Cuba.

In "Posters: Advertisement, Art, Political Artifact, Commodity," included in *The Art of Revolution,* edited by Dugald Stermer (New York: McGraw-Hill, 1970, vii–xxiii)), Sontag situated her reading of Cuban posters in terms of how this genre began as commercial art but was soon adapted to fine art by French artists and others for their own aesthetic and ironic purposes. Posters had always been associated with causes and social movements, she noted in a discussion of World War I patriotic posters, before pivoting to a discussion Cuban posters aimed at "firing moral sympathies rather than promoting private appetites." Compared to contemporary avant-garde French political posters, the Cuban variety tended to be straightforward and understated. Once again Sontag invoked the idea of "pleasure" in the Cuban articulation of "complex moral ideas," attitudes, and "ennobling historical references." She did recognize, however, that for the individual artist the sociocultural element of posters could be problematic: How to be part of a revolutionary society and still maintain an individual vision and art? Then she shifted the ground of her argument to suggest that Cuban posters reflected revolutionary internationalist values as opposed to the socialist realism of conforming Soviet artists. And unlike fascist posters, Cuban posters did not seek to "purify" or "glorify" a nationalist culture. She doubted whether a revolutionary poster art could survive in a capitalist society, where poster art was a "mass addiction."

Sontag's mention of Stockholm in her *Ramparts* article about the Cuban revolution reflected her nearly two-year stay in Sweden to work on two films, *Duet for Cannibals* and *Brother Carl.* Although Stockholm might have seemed like a model society for Sontag to tout when decrying American provincialism, in fact in "A Letter from Sweden" (*Ramparts,* July 1969, 23–38), her disaffection with her Scandinavian sojourn is evident. She found the Swedes complacent. Compared to Americans, Swedes seemed even more isolated and passive. They seemed to think very little about the implications of their behavior, as if they were deliberately avoiding any sort of conflict. Alcoholism was one of the few ways repressed Swedes could let out their feelings. Otherwise they appeared to have a mania for locking things up—another sign of their repression. Underlying such behavior was a pervasive anxiety that made conversation difficult and was only relieved by their love of nature. This last point is a curious one, perhaps saying as much about Sontag as about the Swedes, since she had almost no feeling for nature, no understanding of how it functioned as a constituent of the human psyche. Even the tepid nature of Swedish pornography offended her. Compared to Japanese erotica, the Swedish variety was "anti-erotic." Not even

Swedish food got a good review. Its bland flavors reflected the conflicted nature of Swedish reactions to sensuality. Swedish socialism was hardly more appealing. If it eschewed the competitiveness of capitalism, it was not based on any genuine cooperative spirit. This virtually soporific society only awakened in its protests against the Vietnam war, which galvanized Swedes to make common cause with the New Left. This passionate commitment to protest was one of the few outlets Swedes permitted themselves; otherwise they were in a chronic state of depression.

Sontag's grim view of Sweden is reflected in the films she made there, especially in her view of the cannibalistic nature of radical politics, which she saw as a primitive, raw desire for power. Primitivism in both its historical and cultural dimensions fascinated Sontag, as is shown in her entry on "Primitivism" for the *Encyclopaedia Britannica* (vol. 18, 1970, 531–32), in which she explored how attitudes toward nature define the idea of the primitive. She discussed the idealization of nature in the Greco-Roman world, the corruption of nature in the Garden of Eden story, and the conflict-ridden working out of the classical and Christian traditions in medieval culture, which viewed nature as part of a corrupt creation and, in turn, expressed an anti-intellectual attitude that rejected the classical notion of nature as the source of wisdom. She then explored how in later periods Romantic writers invested primitivism with a liberating power that was expressed in widely different ways by Rousseau, Nietzsche, Wordsworth, Freud, Artaud, and Picasso.

In "The Double Standard of Aging" (*Saturday Review,* September 23, 1972, 29–38), Sontag began to explore ideas about the plight of women that she later developed in her play *Alice in Bed* and in her introduction to *Women,* Annie Leibovitz's collection of photographs. A woman's age, and how that age is interpreted, Sontag contended, differs from responses to a man's age—no matter whether the society was pre- or postindustrial. And no matter which society is examined, responses to aging are "much more a social judgment than a biological eventuality." For women their sexual attractiveness is a matter of their youth, and women beyond the age of thirty-five are deemed less desirable even though biologically in the years between thirty-five and fifty they are at their sexual peak. All women, Sontag argued, are actresses in the sense that they are concerned with an image of themselves, with stabilizing that image, since the societal concept of beauty demands that the face and body do not change. Aging female flesh is regarded with horror because what is desirable is the girl, whereas for men at least two attractive standards are possible: the boy and the man. In response to this double standard, women must begin to treat themselves as "full human beings," allowing their faces and bodies to tell the truth about themselves.

Sontag's fullest exploration of female beauty occurs in *The Volcano Lover* in passages about the Cavaliere's wife (Emma Hamilton) whose early beauty captures the imagination of her husband, a connoisseur and collector of beautiful objects but also of "the hero" (Lord Nelson), who falls in love not with the young beauty but with the aging, corpulent Emma. The nature of this couple's intense love fascinated Sontag because even as their society scorns their liaison they remain enraptured with one another. In effect, the hero and the Cavaliere's wife actuate the kind of mutual love that Sontag suggested is nearly impossible because of society's very restricted sense of beauty. Emma's fate, however, is grim: Both her husband, Sir William Hamilton, and her hero, die, leaving her unprotected and no longer immune to society's condemnation. The very uniqueness of her love and life render her unfit by conventional standards, so she must perish alone and despised.

"Susan Sontag Tells How It Feels to Make a Movie" (*Vogue,* July 1974, 118–19) is essentially a promotional piece for her documentary *Promised Lands*. Unlike the writer, she explained, the filmmaker is vulnerable to accidents, the casting of certain actors, funding, and even the weather. Even though *Promised Lands* is a documentary, Sontag saw the film as a reflection of her own sensibility, meaning that there was a continuity between her writing and her work in cinema. Thus the term documentary seemed too narrow when applied to her film. She compared *Promised Lands* to Brechtian drama, which is not plot driven but presents "a condition rather than an action."

Although *Promised Lands* fully reflects the stalemated condition of the Israeli-Palestinian conflict, it also evinces Sontag's belief in a dialogue that could conceivably lead, eventually, to peace. Thus it is not surprising that in "Notes on Optimism," an article in *Vogue* (January 1975, 100, 148, 154), co-authored with her son David Rieff, she argued essentially that optimism can be the only viable position to take, since pessimism is simply an acceptance of the status quo. She saw promising developments in China, North Vietnam, and Cuba in encouraging a sense of community. Similarly, protests against capital punishment as cruel and unusual and women's efforts to lead independent lives suggested to her that it is pointless to take a defeatist attitude, and thus we must act to enforce our beliefs even if we expect the worst.

One of Sontag's least effective pieces is a short article on artist Francis Bacon for *Vogue* (March 1975, 136–37). She believed he was less English than European because of his affinity with the heroic figures of Western painting, including Michelangelo, Titian, Rembrandt, and Goya. The painter's persona was that of the late developer cultivating the aura of the elusive artist, immune to fame. It would seem, in this case, that Sontag was projecting some of her own sensibility, suggesting that the artist's paintings do not have a theme so much as they exemplify "being in pain."

In "A Woman's Beauty: Put-down or Power source?" (*Vogue,* April 1975, 118–19), Sontag returned to the singular way women are measured against a standard of beauty, which encourages self-absorption, dependence, and immaturity. Women are fragmented into parts, making it difficult for them to assess their whole beings. Beauty must be recontextualized, Sontag argued, so as to separate it from the "mythology of the 'feminine.'" How to counter that mythology was the thrust of a follow-up piece, "Beauty: How Will It Change Next?" (*Vogue,* May 1975, 116–17, 174), which noted that ideas of beauty and freedom are incompatible, since beauty is equated with the exceptional and contrasted with what is common. Beauty, in short, is an "ideology," a cultural construct that does not exist in China, for example. That ideology, however, is subverted in the androgynous performances of David Bowie, for example, and the 1960s craving for a "plurality of styles." Sontag extended her discussion of beauty in the lead essay in *Where the Stress Falls.*

Sontag's articles in *Vogue* seem to be, in part, a response to the second wave of feminism that began in the 1970s, although she never associated herself directly with the women's liberation movement and did not adopt its jargon. In "Women: Can Rights be Equal?" (*Vogue,* July 1976, 100–101), Sontag did address a decade of feminist activism, noting that the drive for the Equal Rights Amendment actually suggested the waning powers of the cause. The ERA had been regarded, to begin with, as a reformist measure and hardly the goal of revolutionary feminism, but had since become part of a "front line of struggle." The ERA had symbolic value, but Sontag did not wish to see it become so all important. Most important still was changing the way men and women thought about equal rights.

In an introduction to Peter Hujar's *Portraits in Life and Death* (New York: Da Capo, 1976), Sontag extended the argument she made in *On Photography,* noting the photograph's tendency to romanticize reality so that the ordinary could seem unique. Photography records but it also re-creates the world. Even death becomes a subject of the romantic camera eye, and Hujar's portraits of friends (including Sontag) become posed as part of a meditation on dying. As has often been noted, his photographs of the Palermo Catacombs directly influenced the final scene in *Death Kit.*

Although Sontag's contribution to a symposium published in *Photography within the Humanities,* edited by Eugenia Parry Janis and Wendy MacNeill (Danbury, N.H.: Addison House, 1977, 110–21), repeats the arguments of *On Photography,* Sontag provided a more personal perspective by calling herself a "photograph junkie" who cut photographs out of magazines. She also suggested that an uneasiness about photography's status as an art persists. Even so, its place in a study of the humanities can be crucial since photography can be regarded as a "meta-art . . . where all kinds of sociological and moral and historical questions can be raised." In a related article, "Looking with Avedon" (*Vogue*, September 1978, 461, 507–8), she suggested that fashion photography can become "disinterested, ironic," and a commentary on the "idea of the fashionable." Sontag implied that photography, like film and the other arts, can be a commentary on itself—as is a film like the seven-hour *Hitler, A Film From Germany*, which she also discussed in *Under the Sign of Saturn*. In "Our Hitler: A Masterpiece from Germany" (*Vogue*, May 1980, 256, 325), Sontag suggested that the director was less concerned with the typical documentary filmmaker's concern with the "Hitler-that-was" and more with the contemporary view of him. By focusing on the image of Hitler, Hans Jurgen Syberberg transcended the "primal opposition" between "fiction and documentary" by showing how a culture's perceptions of a figure like Hitler derives from both history and the imagination.

"On Dance and Dance Writing" (*New Performance*, 1981, 72–81), Sontag explored an art form that, in part, grew out of her relations with dancers like Lucinda Childs, who dances in Sontag's film *Unguided Tour*. Sontag believed that choreographers and dancers were producing some of the "best work in the world." As a form of modernism, dance set new standards as defined by some of the best dance criticism written by Edwin Denby, who was especially attuned to the way dancer's bodies are used to create new forms. While dance can be appreciated in terms of abstract form, it is also, like the other arts, the product of specific cultures and artists, so that dance, like the other arts, can also be political.

Sontag's own involvement in politics became the focus of "The Hard Lesson of Poland's Military Coup" (*Los Angeles Times*, February 14, 1982, part IV, 2), in which she excoriated the "so-called democratic left" for not engaging in an honest anti-Communism—in part, because of a response to McCarthyism, which made anti-Communism seem like a reactionary movement. Sontag confessed that she, too, had been reluctant to condemn Communism in a forthright fashion in spite of eloquent testimony from Polish exiles such as Czeslaw Miłosz. Like the rest of the left, she spent too much time trying to "distinguish *among* communisms." The Polish Communism crackdown on the Solidarity union and its supporters showed that Communism was another form of fascism, a truth that the Left had spent too much time denying.

Sontag's speech to students "Be Bold! Be Bold!" (*Realia*, December 1983, 15) reads almost like a coda to her comments on von Stroheim's fate in

Hollywood, since she targeted censorship as a "formal principle" that prevented great art from being created and distributed. What bothered her was the provincialism of censors, which could be countered, she urged, by thinking of art in international terms, which could promote and secure the "existence of liberty."

In "Images of People Past" (*Art and Antiques*, May 1984, 66–67), Sontag contrasted the impact of words and images by examining Paul Nadar's photographs of Proust's contemporaries with passages from Proust's fiction. Whereas Proust could narrate the lives of his characters and provide them with a sensual attraction, Nadar's photographs seemed remote, mask-like. Despite photography's association with the real and concrete, and with stopping time in an image, Proust's words capture the effect of time more decisively than an effort to use photographs to illustrate his narration.

In "Model Destinations" (*TLS*, June 1984, 699–700), Sontag explored the nature of travel in classical, medieval, and modern literature—from the notion of utopia as a travel destination to the ideas of the Romantics, who used travel as way of examining their own mentalities in quest of a paradise lost. She also commented on how modern travelers looked to peasant societies to reflect on the past, on the premodern, and to criticize modern consumer society. Communist governments, well aware of the traveler's desire to find an alternative to their flawed societies, were careful to present only a positive experience. This was a problem she struggled with in "Trip to Hanoi."

In "When Writers Talk among Themselves" (*New York Times Book Review* feature, January 5, 1986, 1, 22–23), Sontag dealt with the contrast between the writer's solitude, when the writing gets done, and the invitations to public events like writers' congresses. Such meetings inevitably raised questions about culture and cultural relations that led writers into the political realm, even though the congresses themselves were supposed to be "beyond politics." To Sontag, the value of such gatherings was the opportunity for writers to converse about their work. When a writer did speak about politics, she noted, the nature of the audience made a key difference—whether it consisted of fellow writers, as in her addresses to writers about Communism and fascism in 1977 and 1980, or nonwriters in 1982, when her words stirred considerable animosity and attacks on her.

"Fragment of an Aesthetic of Melancholy," in *"Veruschka": Trans-figurations* by Vera Lehndorff and Holger Trülzsch (London: Thames and Hudson, 1986, 6–12), reads like an addendum to *Under the Sign of Saturn* and *On Photography*. Sontag's ostensible subject is the actress and model Veruschka, but as the quotation marks in the book's title suggest, it is not Veruschka per se but rather her representation in photographs that is the true concern. The photographs explore the nature of artifice that could both camouflage the self and make that self a spectacle, as in the theatricality of fashion photography, in which clothes painted on a body, so to speak, entomb it, making, in this case, an object out of the actress, who becomes passive and simply part of the form that the photograph captures. And yet setting some of the photographs in the ruins of abandoned industrial and commercial spaces inevitably suggest ruination and desolation, even though Veruschka remains a dynamic figure opposed to traditional representations of a seated Melancholy.

Sontag's preface to *Maria Irene Fornés: Plays* (New York: PAJ Publications, 1986, 7–10), emphasizes the Cuban playwright's "aversion to the reductively psychological"—a stance that Sontag shared. The intellectual quality of Fornés's plays impressed Sontag as well as the playwright's depiction of women's lives and her understanding of history. Even the more realistic plays, Sontag argued, are of a piece with Fornés's "theatre of fantasy."

Politics and cultural commentary merge to some extent in "In Conclusion . . ." (*East-West Journal,* December 1987, 99–106), Sontag's contribution to a conference on humor, which is often defined in the context of particular societies. Folk humor, for example, is related to local, regional, and national traditions. She cited theoreticians such as Bergson, Freud, and Bakhtin, who treated humor as a form of disruptive criticism. How critics react to a film as humorous can say as much about their cultural predispositions as about the film, Sontag noted, when contrasting her view of *Kind Hearts and Coronets* with the reactions of an Indian colleague.

"Pilgrimage" (*New Yorker,* December 21, 1987, 38–40, 50, 53–54) is Sontag's most extended autobiographical essay. It centers on her visit to Thomas Mann. This version of the visit differs markedly from her account in her diary (see chapter eight), relating how, as a high school student, she was cajoled by her friend Merrill into contacting the famous German author living in exile in Los Angeles. The essay contrasts the prisonhood of her childhood and bookish sensibility with the superficial affability of her stepfather and the drivel of the culture around her. She identified with Hans Castorp, the hero of Mann's novel *The Magic Mountain,* and regarded the novel's author as a literary god. So she could not conceive of why Mann would want to meet her. He seemed as remote from her existence as movie stars like Ingrid Bergman and Gary Cooper. But Merrill took the initiative, and Sontag submissively accompanied him to Mann's home, where the students had little to say, and Sontag was shocked by how frail Mann looked in person. Nevertheless, Sontag was able to exercise her passion for music by discussing Wagner and Mann's new book. And at least Sontag was heartened to hear Mann say that *The Magic Mountain* was his greatest novel. In this rendition of tea with a famous author, Sontag portrayed herself as retiring and puzzled as to why Mann was so kind to these nobodies who had looked him up. She also had to agree with Merrill that they hadn't made "total fools" of themselves. The story, and it reads like a story, seems almost a parable about the perils of meeting one's literary idol. It is also a revealing record of Sontag's sense of isolation and inability to share her enthusiasms with others, except for a very few friends. In the end, "Pilgrimage" is about Sontag's quest, her journey to discover literary greatness and to be found worthy of the company of great writers.

Fiction

"Man with a Pain" (*Harper's,* April 1964, 72–75) reads almost like an amalgam of *The Benefactor* and *Death Kit.* The story is set in Manhattan and centers on a protagonist who cannot make his peace with the city. He feels fragmented, his days full of accidents, anxieties, and a sense of isolation, but the story lacks development and is more the description of a condition than a narrative of events—in keeping with Sontag's early rejection of conventional fiction with its well-made plots and characters that fit into the conventions of realism.

"Description (of a Description)" (*Antaeus,* Autumn 1984, 111–14) is another oblique study of a narrative consciousness, given from two perspectives of a man who collapses on a public street. Customary explanations of the man's conditions are thwarted. He cannot be placed certainly in the context of society, or of psychology. Why the man falls and what the fall means are never explained. The last section of the story suggests that he may have been reacting to a love affair, but even the timing of his fall and whether it is a present or future event cannot be known for sure. Is this a story about disintegration, the disintegration of the character and of the narrative that attempts to tell his story?

Like "Description (of a Description)," "The Letter Scene" (*New Yorker,* August 18, 1986, 24–32) is more of a meditation than a narrative. A variation on Scene II of Tchaikovsky's opera *Eugene Onegin,* the story of Tatyana writing a love letter to Eugene receives complex treatment in a multiplicity of voices, including Eugene's as he writes a letter to his father (not included in the opera); thus the nature of the letters themselves and the language that expresses them become the focus of the story, if it can be called that. Allusions to Sontag's divorce from Philip Rieff also call into question the story's status as fiction. Letters can be expressions of love but also "a way of keeping someone at a distance."

"The View from the Ark," in *Violent Legacies: Three Cantos* by Richard Misrach (New York: Aperture, 1992), reads as a kind of framework for Misrach's photographs from a nuclear test site in Nevada. This is yet another experimental fiction unrelated, it seems at first, to the photographs. Sontag's narrator, "one of the descendants of Noah," discusses the nature of storytelling. Then a familiar Sontag theme is explored: the differences between seeing and knowing, between pictures and stories. The theme uniting the disparate parts of Sontag's fiction seems to be the recurrence of "bad news all the time," the announcement that "it's a cruel world out there." Just ignoring this news is what leads to the "pleasure of killing." Notwithstanding these gloomy thoughts, the possibility is raised that the world can be saved by the possibility of imagining it saved—that is, by literature itself. Sontag's abstruse exchanges seem to be a more elaborate way of restating her philosophical belief in optimism, which is expressed directly in her "Notes on Optimism."

NOTES

All references to page numbers in Sontag's texts are from Kindle e-book editions. In one case, *I, etcetera,* location numbers are given in the absence of page numbers.

Chapter 1—Understanding Susan Sontag

1. For the details of Sontag's biography, see Rollyson and Paddock, *Susan Sontag: The Making of an Icon;* Schreiber, *Susan Sontag: A Biography;* and Maunsell, *Susan Sontag.*

2. See Sontag, "Homage to Halliburton," *Where the Stress Falls,* 253–56.

Chapter 2—Early Novels and Essays

1. Michel Mohrt, "Rêve et réalité chez Susan Sontag," in *L'Air du large: Essais sur le roman étranger,* 284–88 (Paris: Gallimard, 1970). Quoted in Poague and Parsons, *Susan Sontag: An Annotated Bibliography,* 346.

2. Sontag, *Where the Stress Falls,* 34.

3. Granville Hicks, "To Act, Perforce to Dream," *Saturday Review,* September 7, 1963, 17–18. See also John Wain, "Song of Myself," *New Republic,* September 21, 1963, 26–27, 30.

4. James R. Frakes, "Where Dreaming Is Believing," *New York Herald Tribune Book Week,* September 22, 1963, 10.

5. Robert M. Adams, "Nacht und Tag," *New York Review of Books,* October 17, 1963, 19.

6. Stephen Koch, "Imagination in the Abstract," *Antioch Review* 24 (Summer 1964): 253–63.

7. Kazin, "Cassandras: Porter to Oates," in *Bright Book of Life: American Novelists and Storytellers from Hemingway to Mailer,* 163–205. Robert W. Flint's review in *Commentary,* (December 1963, 489–90), refers to Sontag's "feminine" assessment, which differs markedly from those of her male contemporaries such as Norman Mailer, James Baldwin, and Joseph Heller.

8. Bruce Bassoff, "Private Revolution: Sontag's *The Benefactor,*" *Enclitic* 3, no. 2 (Fall 1979): 59–73.

9. Ching and Wagner-Lawlor, *The Scandal of Susan Sontag,* 9.

10. I'm grateful to Bernard F. Rodgers Jr. for sharing his unpublished manuscript with me. Theodore Solotaroff, "Death in Life," *Commentary,* November 1967, 87–89; Burton Feldman, "Evangelist of the New," *Denver Quarterly* 1 (Spring 1966): 152–56.

11. See Sontag, preface to *Reborn.*

12. Solotaroff, "Death in Life," 87–89.

13. Reviews of *Death Kit:* Eliot Fremont-Smith, *New York Times,* 31; Doris Grumbach, *America,* August 26, 1967, 207; Richard Lehan, *Contemporary Literature,* Autumn 1968, 538–53.

14. Sontag, *As Consciousness Is Harnessed to Flesh,* 234–35.

15. Ibid.

16. John Leonard, "Susan Sings in a Lonely Thicket," *Life,* March 28, 1969, 12.

17. Christopher Lehmann-Haupt, "Susan Sontag and the Life of the Mind," *New York Times,* May 2, 1969, 41.

18. John Weightman, "High Modernist Critic," *Observer* (London), November 30, 1969, 34; Jonathan Raban, "The Uncourtly Muse," *New Statesman,* December 12, 1969, 866–67.

19. Sontag, "Speaking Freely," in Poague, *Conversations with Susan Sontag,* 7.

Chapter 3—Photography and Film

1. Howard Kissel, "Susan Sontag—She's Not Choosing Sides," *Women's Wear Daily,* July 8, 1974, 24.

2. Stanley Kauffmann, *New Republic,* June 29, 1974, 18, 33–34.

3. Reviews of *Promised Lands:* Nora Sayre, *New York Times,* July 12, 1974, 44; David Moran, *Boston Phoenix,* August 6, 1974, sections 2 and 8; Byron Stuart, "Jews Understand Drama, Not Tragedy," *Real Paper* (Cambridge, Mass.), August 7, 1974; John Simon, *Esquire,* October 1974, 14, 16, 20, 24.

4. See also *On Photography,* 7, 81.

5. Reviews of *On Photography:* Ben Lifson, "An Eloquent Distortion," *Village Voice,* November 28, 1977, 44–45; Edward Grossman, "False Images," *Saturday Review,* December 10, 1977, 46–48; Candace Leonard, "The Soft Addiction," *Et Cetera,* Winter 1978, 442–45: Alfred Kazin, "Sontag Is Not a Camera," *Esquire,* February 1978, 50–51; Harvey Green, *Winterthur Portfolio,* Summer 1979, 209–11; Laurie Stone, "On Sontag," *Viva,* November 1978, 39–40; Paul Lewis, "On Sontag," *Ten.8,* Summer 1979, 3.

6. Reviews of *On Photography:* William Gass, "A Different Kind of Art," *New York Times Book Review,* December 18, 1977, 7, 30, 33; Michael Starenko, "On *On Photography,*" *New Art Examiner,* April 1978, 12, 23; Rudolf Arnheim, *Journal of Aesthetics and Art Criticism,* Summer 1978, 514–15; John Simon, "Looking Into The Camera," *New Leader,* February 13, 1978, 17–18; Robert Melville, "Images of the Instant Past: Sontag on Photography, *Encounter,* November 1978, 69–73.

7. Poague, *Conversations with Susan Sontag,* 132.

8. Fourteen highlighters as of October 2014 when I downloaded the book to my Kindle.

9. Twenty-nine highlighters as of October 2014 when I downloaded the book to my Kindle.

10. Reviews of *Regarding the Pain of Others:* Peter Conrad, "What the Eye Can't See," *Observer* (London), August 2, 2003, http://www.theguardian.com/theobserver/2003/aug/03/society; John Leonard, "Regarding the Pain of Others," *New York Times,* March 23, 2003, http://www.nytimes.com/2003/03/23/books/review/023LEONAT.html. See also Lopate, *Notes on Sontag,* 212.

11. Peter M. Stevenson, "Leibovitz Sees Glitz and Grit, Sontag Broods on the Big Idea," *New York Observer,* November 8, 1999, http://observer.com/1999/11/leibovitz-sees-glitz-and-grit-sontag-broods-on-the-big-idea/.

Chapter 4—Illness and its Metaphors

1. Reviews of *Illness as Metaphor:* William Logan, "Exploring the Fantasies and Ritual Fears of Disease," *Chicago Tribune Book World,* June 11, 1978, 1; Maggie Scarf, "A Message from the Kingdom of the Sick," *Psychology Today,* July 1978, 111–12, 114, 116; Dennis Donoghue, "Disease Should Be Itself," *New York Times Book Review,* July 16, 1978, 9, 27; A. Alvarez, "Diseased Imaginations," *Observer* (London), February 18, 1979, 37.

2. Reviews of *Illness as Metaphor:* John Leonard, *New York Times,* June 1, 1978, C19; Walter Clemons, "Mythology of Illness," *Newsweek,* June 12, 1978, 96D; Geoffrey Wolff, "Diffusing the Rhetoric of a Dread Disease," *New Times,* July 10, 1978, 74–75.

3. Reviews of *AIDS and its Metaphors:* Christopher Lehmann-Haupt, "Shaping the Reality of AIDS through Language," *New York Times,* January 16, 1989, C18; Charles Perrow, "Healing Words," *Chicago Tribune Books,* January 22, 1989, 6; Randy Shilts, "Insights into an Epidemic of Fear," *Sunday San Francisco Examiner and Chronicle Review,* January 29, 1989, 1, 11; Jan Zita Grover, "AIDS Culture," *Women's Review of Books,* April 1989, 5–6.

4. Maunsell, *Susan Sontag,* e-book edition, location 2097.

5. Reviews of "The Way We Live Now": Gardner McFall, *New York Times Book Review,* March 1, 1992, 20; Barbara MacAdam, "Speaking of the Unspeakable," *Artnews,* March 1992, 20; Rosemary Dinnage, "Learning How to Die," *TLS,* March 22, 1991, 19.

Chapter 5—The Voices of Fiction: Stories and Later Novels

1. Poague and Parsons, *Susan Sontag: An Annotated Bibliography, 1948–1992,* 94.

2. Reviews of *I, etcetera:* Anatole Broyard, "Styles of Radical Sensibility," *New York Times,* November 11, 1978, 21; Daphne Merkin, "Getting Smart," *New Leader,* December 18, 1978, 12–13; Todd Gitlin, "Sontag's Stories," *Progressive,* March 1979, 58–59; Anne Tyler, *New Republic,* November 25, 1978, 29–30.

3. Reviews of *The Volcano Lover:* Daniel Max, "Tricky Nelson and the Lady," *Wall Street Journal,* July 30, 1992, A11; A. S. Byatt, "Love and Death in the Shadow of Vesuvius," *Washington Post Book World,* August 16, 1992, 1–2; Michiko Kakutani, "History Mixed with Passion and Ideas," *New York Times,* August 4, 1992, C16; Maria Warner, "On Naples, Love, and Lava," *Vogue,* August 1992, 148; John Banville, "By Lava Possessed," *New York Times Book Review,* August 9, 1992, 26–27; David Slavitt, "Susan Sontag Creates a Bold Historical Romance That Finally Mocks Itself," *Chicago Tribune Books,* August 9, 1992, 4, 6; Richard Eder, "That Hamilton Woman," *Los Angeles Times Book Review,* August 16, 1992, 3, 7.

4. Reviews of *The Volcano Lover:* Rhoda Koenig, "Past Imperfect, Future Wacked-Out," *New York,* August 17, 1992, 50–52; Jonathan Keates, "The Antique Collector's Guide," *TLS,* September 25, 1992, 24; Evelyn Toynton, "The Critic as Novelist," *Commentary,* November 1992, 62–64; R. Z. Sheppard, "Lava Soap," *Time,* August 17, 1992, 66–67; L. S. Klepp, "Kingdom of Excess," *Entertainment Weekly,* August 21, 1992, 52; David Gates, "There is No Crater Love," *Newsweek,* August 24, 1992, 63; John Simon, "The Valkyrie of Lava," *National Review,* August 31, 1992, 63–65; Francis L. Bardacke, "The Hero and the Beauty," *San Diego Magazine,* November 1992, 62, 64; Bernard F. Rodgers, *Magill's Literary Annual 1993,* 856–59.

5. Doreen Carvajal, "So Whose Words Are They? Susan Sontag Creates a Stir," *New York Times,* May 27, 2000, http://partners.nytimes.com/library/books/052700sontag -america.html. See also *Worry Later* blog, http://worrylater.blogspot.com/2011/08/susan -sontags-plagiarism-few.html.

6. The letters from Sontag's lovers and admirers will be discussed in the forthcoming revised and updated edition of Carl Rollyson and Lisa Paddock's *Susan Sontag: The Making of an Icon.* For Joseph Cornell's interest in Sontag, see Rollyson and Paddock, 94–96.

7. Reviews of *In America:* Sarah Kerr, "Diva," *New York Times Book Review,* March 2, 2000, https://www.nytimes.com/books/00/03/12/reviews/000312.12kerrlt.html; Michiko Kakutani, "'In America': Love as a Distraction That Gets In the Way of Art," *New York Times,* February 29, 2000, https://www.nytimes.com/library/books/022900 sontag-book-review.html; John Sutherland, "Excess Baggage," *Guardian,* June 9, 2000, http://www.theguardian.com/books/2000/jun/10/fiction.reviews3; James Woods, "The Palpable Past-Intimate," *New Republic,* March 7, 2000, http://www.powells.com/ review/2001_07_26; Elaine Showalter, *New Statesman,* June 5, 2000, http://www.new statesman.com/node/137834; Michael Silverblatt, "For You O Democracy," *Los Angeles Times Book Review,* February 27, 2000, 1–2.

8. Adam Begley, "Sontag's High-Tone Tale: Her Brains Center Stage," *New York Observer,* February 28, 2000, http://observer.com/2000/02/sontags-hightoned-tale -her-brains-center-stage/.

Chapter 6—Experiments in Theater

1. See Julia A. Walker, "Sontag and Theater," in Ching and Wagner-Lawler, *The Scandal of Susan Sontag,* 128–54.

2. The text for *A Parsifal* can be found online at *Scribd.,* http://www.scribd.com/ doc/216872405/Susan-Sontag-A-Parsifal#scribd.

3. Yuval Sharon, review for the Wagner Society of New York, http://www.yuval sharon.com/Sontag%20A%20Parsifal.pdf.

4. Charles Isherwood, "Wagner Didn't Write an Opera for a Talking Ostrich, Did He?," *New York Times,* March 1, 2006, http://www.nytimes.com/2006/03/01/theater/ reviews/01pars.html.

5. Walker, "Sontag and Theater," 140.

6. Marie Olesen Urbanski, "A Festering Rage," *Los Angeles Times,* October 10, 1993, http://www.nytimes.com/2006/03/01/theater/reviews/01pars.html; David Finkle, "Alice in Bed," *Theater Mania,* December 4, 2000, http://www.theatermania.com/new -york-city-theater/reviews/12-2000/alice-in-bed_1144.html.

7. Rollyson and Paddock, *Susan Sontag: The Making of an Icon,* 295.

8. Quoted in Walker, "Sontag and Theater," 149.

Chapter 7—Impresario of Modern Literature

1. I saw such a Goodman performance at Michigan State University when, as an undergraduate, I attended his public lecture.

2. Reviews of *Under the Sign of Saturn:* John Leonard, *New York Times,* October 13, 1980, C22; Seymour Krim, "Susan Sontag: Shifting from High to Low Gear," *Chicago Tribune Book World,* October 19, 1980, 3; John Lahr, "Box Seat at the Theater of Ideas," *Washington Post Book World,* October 26, 1980, 3, 14; Frank Kermode, "Alien Sages," *New York Review of Books,* November 6, 1980, 42–43; Jonathan Rosenbaum,

"Under the Sign of Sontag," *Soho News,* November 12–18, 1980, 16; David Bromwich, "Large and Dangerous Subjects," *New York Times Book Review,* November 23, 1980, 38–39; Jon Cook, "Six to One," *New Statesman,* September 2, 1983, 22–23; Adrienne Rich and Susan Sontag, "Feminism and Fascism: An Exchange," *New York Review of Books,* March 20, 1975, 31.

3. Frances Spalding (*New Statesman,* January 21, 2002, 48–49) wrote an admiring review of *Where the Stress Falls,* while noting that Sontag's politics and her emphasis on great writers, which showed little interest in literary theory, had turned the academic establishment against her. In the *Women's Review of Books,* October 2001, 4–5, Deborah L. Nelson noted that, with the exception of the essay on Lucinda Childs, Sontag spent little time on female artists, and that this "idiosyncratic" writer seemed disaffected and no longer centrally located in the culture as she was in her earlier work. In the *New York Times Book Review* (November 4, 2001, 7), William Deresiewicz regarded Sontag's book as a "major cultural event," and yet the tone of his review suggests that she had lost a good deal of her audience and her ability to make an impact on contemporary culture.

4. Robert Boyers, "The Devoted," *Harper's,* February 2007, 87–92.

Chapter 8—The Diaries

1. E-mail from Jillian Cuellar, UCLA Special Collections, to Carl Rollyson, January 12, 2014.

2. Sontag dated this entry January 3, 1951, but as David Rieff notes, she was married in January 1950.

3. I heard Sontag extol *An American Tragedy* in a talk given at a literary conference in Poland in 1980.

Chapter 9—The Legacy

1. "One Hundred Years One Hundred Thinkers: Philosophy," *New Republic,* http://www.newrepublic.com/feature/thinkers/literary-criticism/.

BIBLIOGRAPHY

Works by Susan Sontag

Against Interpretation, and Other Essays. New York: Farrar, Straus and Giroux, 1966.
AIDS and Its Metaphors. New York: New York: Farrar, Straus and Giroux, 1989.
Alice in Bed: A Play in Eight Scenes. New York: Farrar, Straus and Giroux, 1993.
As Consciousness Is Harnessed to Flesh: Journals and Notebooks, 1963–1980. Edited by
   David Rieff. New York: Farrar, Straus and Giroux, 2012.
At the Same Time: Essays and Speeches. Edited by Paolo Dilonardo and Anne Jump.
   New York: Farrar, Straus and Giroux, 2007.
The Benefactor, a Novel. New York: Farrar, Straus and Giroux, 1963.
Brother Carl. New York: Farrar, Straus and Giroux, 1974.
Death Kit. New York: Farrar, Straus and Giroux, 1967.
Duet for Cannibals. New York: Farrar, Straus and Giroux, 1970
Essays of the 1960s and 70s. Edited by David Rieff. New York: Library of America,
   2013.
I, etcetera. New York: Farrar, Straus and Giroux, 1978.
Illness as Metaphor. New York: Farrar, Straus and Giroux, 1978.
In America. New York: Farrar, Straus, and Giroux, 1999.
On Photography. New York: Farrar, Straus and Giroux, 1977.
"Pilgrimage." *New Yorker,* December 21, 1987, 38–54.
Reborn: Journals and Notebooks, 1947–1963. Edited by David Rieff. New York: Farrar,
   Straus and Giroux, 2008.
Regarding the Pain of Others. New York: Farrar, Straus and Giroux, 2003.
Styles of Radical Will. New York: Farrar, Straus and Giroux, 1969.
A Susan Sontag Reader. Introduction by Elizabeth Hardwick. New York: Farrar, Straus
   and Giroux, 1982.
Under the Sign of Saturn. New York: Farrar, Straus and Giroux, 1980.
The Way We Live Now. London: Jonathan Cape, 1991.
Where the Stress Falls: Essays. New York: Farrar, Straus, and Giroux, 2001.

Secondary Sources

Bergman, David, ed. *Camp Grounds: Style and Homosexuality.* Amherst: University of
   Massachusetts Press, 1993.
Bruss, Elizabeth W. *Beautiful Theories: The Spectacle of Discourse in Contemporary
   Criticism.* Baltimore: Johns Hopkins University Press, 1982.
Ching, Barbara, and Jennifer A. Wagner-Lawlor, eds. *The Scandal of Susan Sontag.* New
   York: Columbia University Press, 2009.

Cott, Jonathan. *Susan Sontag: The Complete Rolling Stone Interview.* New Haven, Conn.: Yale University Press, 2013.

Dawid, Annie. "The Way We Teach Now: Three Approaches to AIDS Fiction." In *AIDS: The Literary Response,* edited by Emmanuel S. Nelson, 197–203, 218. New York: Twayne 1992.

Field, Edward. *The Man Who Would Marry Susan Sontag.* Madison: University of Wisconsin Press, 2005.

Green, Jonathan. *American Photography: A Critical History 1945 to the Present.* New York: Harry N. Abrams, 1984.

Hellman, John. *American Myth and the Legacy of Vietnam.* New York: Columbia University Press, 1986.

Howe, Irving. *The Decline of the New.* New York: Harcourt, Brace, 1970.

Jacobson, Julius. "Reflections on Fascism and Communism." In *Socialist Perspectives,* edited by Phyllis Jacobson and Julius Jacobson, 119–54. Princeton, N.J.: Karz-Cohl Publishing, 1983.

Jeffords, Susan. "Susan Sontag." In *Modern American Critics since 1955.* Vol. 67 of *Dictionary of Literary Biography,* edited by Gregory S. Jay. Detroit: Gale Research, 1988.

Kaplan, Alice. *Dreaming in French: The Paris Years of Jacqueline Bouvier Kennedy, Susan Sontag, and Angela Davis.* Chicago: University of Chicago Press, 2012.

Karl, Frederick R. *American Fictions, 1940–1980: A Comprehensive History and Critical Evaluation.* New York: Harper and Row, 1983.

Kazin, Alfred. *Bright Book of Life: American Novelists and Storytellers from Hemingway to Mailer.* Boston: Little, Brown, 1973.

Kennedy, Liam. *Susan Sontag: Mind as Passion.* Manchester, U.K.: Manchester University Press, 1995.

Krupnick, Mark. "Criticism as an Institution." In *The Crisis of Modernity: Recent Critical Theories of Culture and Society in the United States and West Germany,* edited by Guner H. Lenz and Kurt L. Shell, 156–76. Boulder, Colo.: Westview Press, 1986.

Leibovitz, Annie. *A Photographer's Life, 1990–2005.* New York: Random House, 2006.

Lopate, Phillip. *Notes on Sontag.* Princeton, N.J.: Princeton University Press, 2009.

Maunsell, Jerome Boyd. *Susan Sontag.* London: Reaktion Books, 2014.

McCreadie, Marsha. "The Theorists: Susan Sontag, Annette Michelson, Maya Deren, Hortense Powdermaker, and Claude-Edmond Magny." In *Women and Film: The Critical Eye,* 80–95. New York: Praeger, 1983.

Mileur, Jean-Pierre. *The Critical Romance: The Critic as Reader, Writer, Hero.* Madison: University of Wisconsin Press, 1990.

Nelson, Cary, *The Incarnate Word: Literature as Verbal Space.* Urbana: University of Illinois Press, 1973.

Nunez, Sigrid. *Sempre Susan: A Memoir of Susan Sontag.* New York: Atlas and Co., 2011.

Poague, Leland, ed. *Conversations with Susan Sontag.* Jackson: University Press of Mississippi, 1995.

Poague, Leland, and Kathy A. Parsons. *Susan Sontag: An Annotated Bibliography 1948–1992.* New York: Garland, 2000.

Rieff, David. *Swimming in a Sea of Death: A Son's Memoir.* New York: Simon and Schuster, 2008.

Rodgers, Bernard F., Jr. "Passionate Partiality: Susan Sontag." In *Voices and Visions: Selected Essays,* 127–45. Lanham, Md.: University Press of America, 2001.

―――. "Susan Sontag." Unpublished book manuscript. Courtesy of Bernard F. Rodgers Jr.

Rollyson, Carl. *Female Icons: Marilyn Monroe to Susan Sontag.* New York: iUniverse, 2005.

―――. *Reading Susan Sontag: A Critical Introduction to Her Work.* Chicago: Ivan R. Dee, 2001.

Rollyson, Carl, and Lisa Paddock. *Susan Sontag: The Making of an Icon.* New York: W. W. Norton, 2000.

Sayres, Sohnya. *Susan Sontag: Elegiac Modernist.* London: Routledge, 1990.

Schor, Esther H. "Susan Sontag." In *Modern American Women Writers,* edited by Elaine Showalter, Lea Baechler, and A. Walton Litz, 471–84. New York: Scribner's, 1991.

Schreiber, Daniel. *Susan Sontag: A Biography.* Evanston, Ill.: Northwestern University Press, 2014.

Seligman, Craig. *Sontag and Kael: Opposites Attract Me.* New York: Counterpoint, 1994.

Showalter, Elaine. *Sexual Anarchy: Gender and Culture at the Fin de Siècle.* New York: Viking Penguin, 1990.

Tanner, Tony. *City of Words: American Fiction 1950–1970.* New York: Harper and Row, 1971.

Taylor, Benjamin. "A Centered Voice: Susan Sontag's Short Fiction." *Georgia Review* 34 (Winter 1980): 907–16.

INDEX

142

INDEX